MW01234151

THE
MESSENGER

Part One: *Remembrance and Awakening*

Ivan Taub

authorHOUSE

1663 LIBERTY DRIVE, SUITE 200
BLOOMINGTON, INDIANA 47403
(800) 839-8640
www.authorhouse.com

First published by AuthorHouse 12/06/04

ISBN: 1-4184-0658-9 (e)
ISBN: 1-4184-0657-0 (sc)

Library of Congress Control Number: 2004092338

Printed in the United States of America
Bloomington, Indiana

This book is printed on acid-free paper.

CONTENTS

PRELUDE

NOW

My name is Jonathan West and in all the ways that really matter I am much like you. Like you, I have a tale to tell, and it is one you may have heard, for traveling along the meandering road I have told it many times to both friend and stranger alike. My tale, for some, will be one of doubt and recognition, fear and wonder; for others it will signify an evolving journey of transformation and a vision of a possible future, a future we are co-creating in the manifest domain of consciousness.

I could begin my story with the details of my birth and the events of my childhood, and all the little things that make me who I am. I could even begin with my death. For in truth, my lower self died many times before I became aware that I even had a story worth telling. But because this story, above all else, is a story of hope and love, it must begin at a time of youth, when the spirit, longing for one enduring moment of ecstacy, dances madly on the razor thin edge of the bottomless pit and thinks it will not fall.

And so, my story begins in the summer of 1970, when I was a brash and reckless poet of twenty-four, traveling through Europe with Gina Angelo. Gina had just turned twenty-one and those first few days in Amsterdam sent us into a love-heat.

GINA'S CANTATA

The elements, the conscious life, the mind,
The unseen vital forces, the nine great gates
Of the body; or the five domain of the sense.
Desire, dislike, pleasure and pain, and thought
Deep-woven, and persistency of being;
These all are wrought on matter by the soul.

Bhagavad-Gita

THEN

Holed up in a tiny room overlooking the Stadhouderskade canal, we went at it like scorpions and monkeys until the world went opaque. All that remained was the frantic yelping and clawing, the pressing of flesh and the twisting of torsos, the suctioning, mind-bending spins into the inner and outer reaches, and the starburst penetrations that give way to the draining emptiness that swallows you up and lets you hide from yourself. We were a half-blind pair of reptiles thought extinct for a million years trying to resurrect the whole species in the steamy swamp of our bed. It was a glorious and delicious fever; and then the fever passed and I fell into a deep, dream-like trance.

I saw myself standing on a high cliff overlooking the Caribbean Sea, transfixed by the vast encompassing wetness. The sky was soaked in a gray mist and, behind me, the crumbling walls of an ancient city rose up against a jungle alive with the screams of invisible monkeys. The trees stood like exhausted lovers yearning for the sun's first kiss, and the macaws listened for God in the immeasurable moment when night becomes day and the past becomes the promise of tomorrow. The air was sweet; it kissed the treetops and moved the leaves like shadows over a sky dipped in dreams. And in that dreamy sweetness, I heard an indescribably beautiful voice call to me like a lover in the moonlight, slowly, deliberately, as if time had stopped and the delicate peal of star-chimes signaled the beginning of a new life.

> "There is something you must remember that you have forgotten, something that will make sleep impossible, something that will set a fire burning in your soul and make the oceans evaporate.
>
> "Do you know that God is the fire burning in your soul? Do you know that God is the first thought

you had before you imagined you were something
separate and apart from everything else?

"Do you know that God is the Source of Light,
the Ground of Life, and the Essence of the Self-
Aware Mind? God is that from which you came
and that to which you will return."

As the awe-inducing voice trailed off into space, I felt a warm,
vibrating pulsation deep in my solar plexus, and instantaneously
a shooting star streaked across the indigo sky. In its blazing
incandescence I saw a reflection of Gina, and then as the trailing
star-spark disappeared in the glistening blackness, a crackling
sizzle fired away like a cache of neurons in some infinitesimal
convolution of my brain. There was a flip-flop of Space and
Time, and I was no longer standing above the Caribbean Sea,
but back in Amsterdam, back in the tiny room overlooking the
Stadhouderskade canal, back in the steamy swamp of our bed
pressing Gina against me as we soared upward on the warm,
wet, woozy wind. Higher and higher we flew, losing our way and
ourselves, until we were bound together like twin stars burning
brightly in the heavens.

In that all-consuming light, we saw the spirits of Humankind
intertwined in Celestial Splendor. Yet in the midst of our love,
I was taken with the thought that we were participating in a
forbidden and secret ceremony. Gina was the Earth and I was the
Sun, and the fire that consumed us had both the power to save and
to destroy.

In the flickering candlelight, Gina became a vision of soft,
warm luminescence. I knelt down before her, and it seemed to me
that I had never seen such perfection. I moved up and down and
over her, again and again, breaking through the barriers of our
earthly form and consciousness, until we melted into one body
and one soul. Our love had penetrated every pore of our existence;

for this was a love not for a day or a year, but an unconditional love for all time.

Then I felt Gina's kiss sweep over me like a flaming caress, and with that kiss came an urgent anticipation that demanded release. We were swimming in a sea of ecstatic energy that brought us back and forth through a rush of time, back and forth through a galaxy of lifetimes, back and forth until the instant of surrender gave birth to a thousand shooting stars and the final stillness of exhaustion and emptiness.

We've been in Amsterdam for about a week, and now that the fire has cooled down we've slipped into a nice little groove. Each morning, we put on cut-off jeans and white shirts with the logo of a red pony embroidered on the breast pocket that Gina says gives us a little class, and head out for a stroll.

This morning we ate breakfast in a sunny sidewalk cafe near the Rijksmuseum Museum drinking aperitifs and nibbling pink salmon canapés. We sat beneath a large red-and-white striped umbrella, enthralled by each other and the buoyant laughter of people at play, people who really seemed to know how to enjoy the beauty of the day. Out of those hundreds of people no one was more alive and animated than Gina. Maybe it was leaving Philadelphia or getting away from her family, but whatever the reason, Gina was liberated and her eyes had a lascivious sparkle. It was hard to imagine she was the same demure grad student of art history I had met just a few months ago, the same doe-eyed girl who as a child had dreamt of becoming a nun and dedicating herself to God.

In my own way, just like Gina, I too had been possessed by spiritual longings since childhood. But oddly enough, my first mystical experience came while walking to the playground with my brother and sister. We had just moved into the neighborhood, and, like robots, followed the other kids who lived on the block. I remember passing by a gigantic stone building and looking up at a breathtaking series of stained glass windows. I couldn't have been more than six or seven and didn't know who the people in the glass pictures were or what they were doing, but I stood there transfixed by the dazzling colors. Suddenly, I heard this chorus of voices emanating from the shimmering glass. I couldn't understand what they were singing, yet it sounded familiar, like a name I had always known singing in my soul. The power of the harmony set off an explosion of shudders that ran up the base of my spine and throttled my brain. I'm not certain how long I was immersed in this state of wonder, but eventually I became aware of a singularly beautiful voice that penetrated every cell of my being with a sound more lovely than any imaginable instrument.

As I heard the indescribable voice fill my every pore with awe and wonder, I became aware and convinced that something existed that was very powerful and beyond my small range of understanding, something that had a special role to play in my life and in the life of the world. For an instant, time dissolved, and I saw a face that filled my soul with love smiling at me across an infinity of space. Then, just as I began sinking into bliss, I heard Gina's voice calling to me from the other side of the universe, catapulting me back into reality.

"Hello? Earth calling Jonny. . . anyone out there?"

"Wow," I muttered, shaking my head, "I was really, really gone . . . how'd you know?"

"I'm psychic," Gina said impishly. "C'mon, anybody could tell. I mean you're here . . . but not *quite* here. Like you've drifted off into some kind of spaced-out zone. What's happening?"

"Kind of hard to explain."

"C'mon, c'mon . . . give it a try."

"Well, I was thinking about something that happened to me when I was a boy, and suddenly I found myself experiencing a . . . Presence, a Glorious Presence that's realer than this moment. But the instant I heard your voice and became consciously aware of my thoughts and feelings, it disappeared. I can't quite remember what happened, but I feel as if I was on the verge of understanding something really special."

"Well, what else do you remember?" Gina said, trying to draw me out.

"A face, with peaceful eyes."

"And then?"

"Some voices," I stammered, shifting uncomfortably in my seat.

"And . . . what were those voices doing?"

"I think they were . . . singing."

"Singing?"

"More like chanting."

"Chanting?" Gina said, squinting her eyes quizzically.

"Yeah. Maybe a name, or a prayer."

"What did it sound like?"

I paused for a second and heard myself say: "Like a mysterious song from a faraway place and time."

"OK, *Captain Kirk*," Gina said playfully, giving me a mock Star-Trek salute. "I hear you loud and clear, but what does that mean?" she added with a laugh. "Don't you remember any of the details?"

"No, not really. It's very frustrating."

"Well Jonny," Gina said coyly, "I bet you could remember if you would just relax. Now, close your eyes and start from the beginning. You see a face. There are voices singing . . . chanting; it sounds familiar. Now, what are they saying?"

"I don't know," I said with a surprising sharpness. "I just can't remember, so let's drop it."

"I'm just trying to help," Gina said, tugging at my elbow.

"I know you are," I said apologetically. "But for right now, just let it go. I don't know what more I can say. It's an indescribable feeling you just can't put into words. Like a dream you have again and again, and when you wake up everything's in pieces and nothing makes sense."

"Yeah," Gina mused oddly, "I know the feeling. That's happened to me, too."

"*Really?*" I said with relief. "Now it's your turn. Tell me all about it."

Gina tapped her finger on her chin a few times, gazing upward to show me she was thinking, and then let out with an exuberant rush: "I have this one recurring dream where I'm walking beside a beautiful stream, it's dawn and the sky is full of incredible swirling lights. It's spring, the flowers are all in bloom, the birds are singing, and the joy I'm feeling is almost unbearable. And the sound of all that life - I know this sounds a little crazy - but all of a sudden it sort of merges together and starts speaking to me. It's not exactly a person talking, because I hear it in my thoughts."

"That's not crazy. That's exactly what happens to me. I feel as if something or someone is speaking to me, putting thoughts in my mind. As if I'm on the verge of learning a secret truth that will make me complete and help me make sense of everything that's going on in this freaked-out world of ours. It's a spiritual experience, but at the same time my conscious awareness is heightened; it's so . . . empowering. I know it's really important to sustain the moment, but I can't, and the more I try the quicker it evaporates into nothing. It's as if I'm about to get an answer to a question, a really *Big Question*, one that I've always wanted answered."

At that moment Gina touched my hand tenderly, and as our eyes locked she added, "I know, and if you get this answer, *everything* is going to change."

A deep silence passed between us after which I found myself leaning forward, speaking in a near-whisper. "Gina, did you ever hear of the ancient Guardians? Many people believe they experienced Cosmic Consciousness and that this transforming experience became the basis of all the great religions. It was even said that some of these Illuminated Beings had special powers."

"Powers? What kind of powers?"

"To heal the sick . . . just like Jesus did, and to predict the future. In fact, some people believed the Guardians possessed a secret knowledge that explained the mystery of life and death."

"We're not supposed to *know* about such things," Gina said bluntly.

"What do you mean by that?"

"Well, when I was a little girl I was taught that people who delved into the secret mysteries were heretics, disbelievers, steeped in evil, that kind of thing."

"*Steeped in evil*?" I said in disbelief, adding hotly, "The Guardians believed that in order to know God you had to experience life to the fullest. That each person had unique struggles to work through and overcome in this world. They believed you had to fight to save your soul, and sometimes that meant *facing* the evil inside yourself . . . that makes sense, doesn't it?"

"It may make sense to you," Gina said nervously, "but who wants to face the evil inside yourself? Who knows what you'd find? Besides, aren't there some things that are just too dangerous to know about. You don't even want to think about them, cause if you do . . . it's straight down to you know where."

"Right," I added incredulously. "*That's it*? That's why no one knows or talks about the Guardians and their secret wisdom?"

"*Maybe*," Gina said whimsically, whirling her fingers round her head like an enchantress, poking me in the ribs after each remark for emphasis. "Or maybe they're still around (poke), passing on their secret knowledge in dreams (poke), contacting people through mystical visions" (poke, poke).

"Yeah, yeah, yeah," I sang out like one of the Beatles, grabbing Gina round the waist and caressing her long dark hair. "And before you really understand what it all means - it's wham, bam - back to the Here and Now."

As Gina fell back into her seat and laughed, I watched the sun reflect off her sparkling white teeth, and marveled at her beauty and vitality. She had a striking Mediterranean profile with smooth olive skin, glistening dark eyes, and hair as thick and lustrous as silk rope. As I leaned over to kiss her, our waiter came over with the check, and through the rose colored glasses on his tray the sun appeared like a scorching disc.

"Gina, I'm *melting*. What do you say? Time to breeze?"

Gina gave me a peculiar look and without answering stretched like a tigress - supple, lean, and taut. I threw some money on the table, and watched as she did a devilish pirouette and spun off into a crowd of admiring strangers. Just looking at her sent a rush of fire up the old Kundalini.

As I hustled to catch up with Gina, I felt incredibly exhilarated. It was like a heady whiff of oxygen at 36,000 feet. Ever since that plane had taken off from Philly, it was as if all the worries and pressures of the world had disappeared. I knew the great economic, religious, and political battles still raged on, but somehow, here in Amsterdam, those troubling realities became insignificant. At first, I found this realization shallow and unsettling, but nonetheless, I could neither deny nor overcome the intoxicating sense of freedom I felt surging through me.

When I caught up to Gina and took her hand, I was almost overcome by the sheer joy of being alive. Everywhere we went people looked at us. They could tell how much we were in love. Gina was the dark, sleek beauty. And me? I had a kind of rugged, clean-shaven, spiffy look, with shoulder-length, light brown hair, and blue eyes. I mean, neither one of us was really caught up in the *looks thing*, yet we knew in a quiet, confident way that we made a striking couple.

It was in this state of carefree abandon that we floated across Dam Square and over to Vondelpark, and that's where we first met the artist, sitting behind his easel, enveloped by blue and yellow tulips, painting the swans as they glided across the pond. We wandered over to look at his work and with that one innocent act started a chain of events that would eventually shatter our perfect universe.

The artist was about forty, tall and nattily dressed with intense green eyes, sunburned cheeks, a clipped salt-and-pepper beard, and closely cropped, ruddy hair. As we watched him mix his paints, he unexpectedly turned and stared directly at Gina. Then, with an affectation so common in men who are certain their opinions are of great significance, he declared: "It's all in the light. The landscape reveals itself in the play of light. Look there - the water seems to melt into the sky."

Gina blushed under his gaze. Clearly his directness had touched her in a way she had not expected. An awkward moment passed while she gathered her thoughts, then trying to sound *intellectual* she said, "So you're working in the tradition of Cezanne and Monet. Isn't that the way they defined the essence of their art, and the reason the critics dismissed them as Impressionists?"

"No, no, no - are you blind?" the artist said in a smug and yet somehow endearing way. "My work is nothing like theirs. All they cared about was the surface movement. I paint the interaction *between* the subject and the light."

Then looking at Gina as if she were the only person in the world he continued softly and intimately, "This brings forth an emotional response that reveals an inner truth and meaning. My work is relational, forcing one to connect with the subject, not cognitively, but existentially."

As he turned back toward his easel, he threw me a quick, condescending glance and added haughtily: "My work has nothing at all in common with those *colorists.*"

Even though I thought this sounded like pretentious babble, he presented his views with such confidence and finality that all I could do was nod ineptly. As the artist continued painting with deft and assured brushstrokes he introduced himself as Willem De Kooning, quickly adding that he wasn't that De Kooning - "the famous abstract hoaxer" - but a distant cousin.

We whiled away the day discussing the art of Manet, Degas, and Renoir, the Romantic poetry of Wordsworth, Shelley, and Keats, and watching De Kooning create his meticulous, brightly detailed, naturalistic sketches. De Kooning was an urbane and accomplished artist, and just being around him made me feel inadequate and inconsequential. Whether it was his abundant charm, worldly sophistication, or the effects of the sparkling white wine we drank with carefree abandon, as the afternoon wore on I could tell that Gina was falling under his spell. As the evening sun disappeared, he casually invited us to join him for dinner. Gina accepted - for both of us.

As we ambled out of the park, Gina walked reverently alongside De Kooning carrying his paints while I followed reluctantly, his easel tucked under my arm. We headed down a broad boulevard and, after a few minutes, crossed over a cobblestone bridge which led to a sumptuous Louis XIV-style house. With the bravado of royalty, De Kooning pushed open the ornate door and we stepped into a huge hall crowned by a spectacular frescoed ceiling. Our host poured some sparkling wine from a Grecian-style decanter and, with drinks in hand, we followed him up a winding marble staircase and through a gilded glass, double door that opened up into a breathtaking studio reverberating with Mozart's exquisite piano concerto in C Major.

De Kooning stood in the midst of his kingdom, dazzling us with theories about the transforming power of Art, the comic genius of Moliere, Shakespeare's exquisite love sonnets, Wagner's mythic operas, and with seeming effortlessness he infused his ranging insights with one recurrent theme: the intoxicating beauty of Woman. His salon served as an indelicate monument to this ideal, for on every wall hung exquisitely rendered paintings of nude models, many in provocative positions.

As Gina studied the paintings she became mesmerized, and for an instant, an ominous shadow passed across her face. De Kooning stood close beside her, explaining his method for capturing the curvilinear movement and inner feelings of his models. Gina stood there looking bewitched, and it was at that very moment that De Kooning's seemingly impromptu remark: "It would be so wonderful to paint you," floated effortlessly into our conversation. De Kooning's *revelation* was followed by a series of sly looks and banter which built up to the inevitable question.

"Pose for me."

"Right now?" Gina blurted out anxiously.

Sensing he had almost won, De Kooning drew his fingers slowly across his brow and blinked his eyes several times, as if he were actually considering withdrawing his offer. Then gesturing with a practiced assuredness, he answered with the perfect mix of encouragement and authority, "Yes, of course. Right now, over there, away from the window, near the palm."

For a second, like a bird in a cage whose door has miraculously sprung open, Gina faltered. She was standing before the dizzying possibility of freedom, peering into the depths, gauging the risks, weighing the consequences. Again, she tottered, and then gathering up her resolve - she flew.

"Like this?"

"Not so stiff," De Kooning coaxed.

"Is this better?"

Adroitly placing one hand on her hip and the other on her shoulder, he purred, "Let the feelings within you emerge."

As Gina shifted her torso forward, she put her wine glass to her lips and licked them seductively. De Kooning let out a short roar of approval: "Yes, that's good, very good."

Backpedaling towards his easel he added, "Now, finish your wine." Then with a devilish glee he yelped, "Careful my dear, you're spilling it all over yourself."

De Kooning threw Gina a thick, fluffy, red towel and she began wiping her neck, her arms, her legs with long lingering strokes. As she bent over and the towel touched her ankles, it felt as if time had stopped. I think we all sensed that this was one of those moments that come along once or twice in your life, when what you do next changes everything.

I stared incredulously as Gina, without a hint of self-consciousness, slowly raised her arms above her head, and let the towel slip from her outstretched fingers to the floor. Then, caught up in the giddy flow of it all, amidst the paint and canvas and empty wine bottles, she began unbuttoning her wet blouse and slipping off her shorts.

I could hardly believe what was happening. I didn't know what to think or say or do, so I just stood there dumbfounded. I felt as if someone had kicked me in the stomach. I was nauseous and dizzy, and a sudden quaking fear came over me that I must be invisible.

Gina had been transformed into a beguiling temptress, and soon was striking the most unbelievably erotic poses against the palm tree. De Kooning, who had peeled off his shirt and flung it across the room, was now painting in a bacchanalian frenzy. Yet, although I was burning with jealousy, I was afraid to do anything that might show just how absurd and ridiculous I felt. I had become a voyeur, an interloper who had stumbled upon a secret rite. I was overcome by shame; and then as I heard their rising laughter my sense of shame began changing into something else. I felt a malevolent heat rising up through me like a shot of adrenaline. In one flashing moment, something dark and ancient, frightening and seductive, passed through my brain like a spike of lightning. In an instant, I found myself at De Kooning's throat, my fingers tight around his neck as he struggled for air. Gina was scratching and kicking me, and as I watched De Kooning's eyes bulge and forehead grow crimson I felt invincible. I wanted to kill him, and that feeling was more powerful and complete than any other sensation I had ever known. But then, just as the life was about to drain out of him I felt my fingers release their stranglehold, and as he dropped to the floor I stood there gloating. There was a long moment of silence as Gina helped De Kooning sit up; ever so slowly he came back to life. The frenzy had subsided and, in its place, a dark, somber curtain of gloom had descended upon us. No one said a word, but the look of icy anger and disbelief on Gina's face spoke volumes of bitter condemnation.

But at that moment, I felt triumphant and powerful, beyond reproach or remorse. I was infused with a terrifying sense of vengeful energy, and they were beneath my contempt or concern. I looked down at them as if they were a pair of insignificant insects trying to hide from the face of the sun. Yet surprisingly, as I watched them huddled together, so weak and ordinary, and so desperate to conceal their nakedness, I was shaken by a crushing sense of pity. It was so overwhelming that I could not bear being near them. So, self-consciously and furtively, I ran from the studio and disappeared into the darkness of the night.

I spent the next few hours wandering remorsefully through the streets, and it was almost dawn when I returned to the hotel. Gina wasn't in our room, so I sat up in bed anxiously waiting for her. Each minute went by torturously, and the minutes turned into maddening hours. It was almost noon when Gina slunk into the room like a ghostly apparition, climbed in beside me, and turned her face to the wall. Eventually, I pulled the covers over my head and tried to go to sleep, but I was too wired for that.

The first few days after the De Kooning episode were very rough. Although we wanted to and needed to, we never spoke about what had happened. One thing was clear, things between us would never be quite the same. In the long run they might turn out better, perhaps much worse, but definitely not the same as they had been. Our idyllic little romance had suddenly taken on a sobering character and we were no longer drunk on love.

Each afternoon, when Gina told me she was going for a walk in the park, I lied and said it was just as well - that it would give me some quiet time to write - but those afternoons were spent in a seething rage, and writing was impossible. I knew Gina was uncontrollably drawn to De Kooning, and no matter how I tried, all I could do was think about them. *Gina and De Kooning*? How was that loathsomeness possible?

Every few minutes, I'd get up from my makeshift desk and look out of the window toward Vondelpark, then I'd pick up a long sharp letter opener off the table and imagine rushing into De Kooning's salon and plunging it deep into their vile writhing flesh. But as the sheer horror of those thoughts throttled me, I'd throw the blade down and try to control my shaking hands. Minutes later, I'd be back at the desk trying to write, but inevitably the dark mood would steal over me and I'd find myself skulking morosely round the room reenacting the murderous scene. It was a twisted and morbid fantasy which I tried to deny, but there was something growing inside of me that was evil and irresistible.

Later that evening, Gina returned to the hotel on the verge of hysteria, her lip cut, her face covered with purplish bruises. At first she was incoherent, but after she calmed down I managed to piece together what had happened. Apparently, she had been drinking in the studio with a few of De Kooning's friends and things got out of control. When she refused to join De Kooning in a threesome, he beat her viciously and threw her out.

De Kooning's hold over Gina had been irrevocably broken, and now she was resting in my arms, telling me how much she loved me, how she had been such a fool, and that she would never again be unfaithful. Soon I was kissing her swollen cheeks and telling her that I would love her forever. Soon her tears were mingled with mine and, at least for the moment, all our dark twisted thoughts and acts were as though they had never existed.

It took about two weeks for Gina's cuts and bruises to heal, but even though she once again appeared radiantly beautiful, the De Kooning affair had left a dark scar on what had been an unblemished heart. As the days went by, she became sullen and withdrawn. We needed something fresh and exciting to come along, and it did. One afternoon while nursing a beer in Dam Square, we heard the vigorous strumming of a guitar and the wailing vocal of Jethro Tull's *Locomotive Breath*. Walking toward us was a tall, blonde, bushy-haired troubadour with a loony grin. As he sang, he shot us a friendly glance and let out a lusty good-natured laugh. I knew right away that this was a fellow traveler on the high road to adventure. As he threw me a quirky nod, he jumped into an old Everly Brothers tune; I supplied the harmony and Gina added some table thumping percussion.

Our musical jam went on like that for maybe ten minutes. When it was over, we knocked off a few beers, found out that the troubadour was a dropout from the University of Wisconsin named Mark Forester, and then started swapping Rock and Roll stories.

Forest, that's what everyone called him, told us about the time he arm-wrestled Jim Morrison at a topless bar in North Beach, and I told him about the time I jammed with Jimi Hendrix when he was still a back-up guitar player. Then he told us about his "roadie days" with Moby Grape, and how he had come to Amsterdam for a three-week gig with a raunchy blues band, and when the gig ended he decided to hang just a *bit* longer. Well, a bit longer turned into a month, and then he got this cool apartment, and then he met this girl, and then *somehow* six months went by, and then he broke up with the girl and got a new apartment, and now he had been here for a year and couldn't think of any reason to leave.

We went on like that for the rest of the afternoon, drinking glass after glass of beer, and as each story got more incredible, Gina would look at us with eye-popping incredulity and say something like, "Is that really true? Did you really do that? You're putting me on, right?" And we'd break out laughing, order another round, and start in with another whopper.

Over the next few days, Gina seemed to regain some of her lost innocence, and with Forest as our guide, we began an exploration of the city. We became well acquainted with the underground jazz clubs in the red-light district, where girls looking as if they had just stepped out of low-budget B-movies, sat provocatively in lingerie, or swayed hypnotically in canal level windows advertising themselves for sex.

One night, for a goof, Forest took us to a dingy cellar of a club where a drunken crowd of losers got on the stage with some prostitutes, and then they brought out this big dog . . . and you know what dogs like to do. Well, you should have seen the look on Gina's face. I thought her eyeballs were gonna pop out of her head!

Anyway, we beat it out of there before much happened and headed over to our favorite hangout: the Milky Way. The Milky Way was like no other place you could imagine. It might have been a warehouse or a market at one time, but now it was a tribal meeting place for runaways, artists, hustlers, gurus, merchants, and drug dealers. It was an emporium of pleasure, thick with the sweet smoke of incense, marijuana, and mind melting hashish. Every nook and corner was jammed with tables displaying clothes in wild jungle colors, records with amoebae-pattern covers, silver jewelry decorated with turquoise and lapis lazuli, and exotic paraphernalia for cleaning, storing, and consuming drugs.

There were pup tents set up everywhere, and you had to watch where you walked because people were camped out haphazardly in sleeping bags. The entire place was an intricate maze pulsating with voices of a dozen different languages and music coming from a thousand different sources. It was a crawling pit of chaos and forbidden delights where you could lose your identity and become whatever you desired. There was no real sense of time in this netherworld; outside it might be ten in the morning or midnight, but inside the Milky Way it was always the same. Once you entered and heard the huge metal door clang behind you, you were transported into another dimension of reality that had its own immutable laws.

Whenever we went into the Milky Way we stayed close to Forest, and tonight was no exception. We followed him as he worked his way through the maze like a Vietnamese soldier sliding through the rice paddies. After a few minutes, he stopped in front of a tall, reed-thin man, dressed like a medieval sorcerer. Directly before him was a small table, and on it about a dozen kinds of hashish and several sets of scales.

After a quick survey I shouted at Forest, "What's that over there, on the end? The one that looks like a chocolate bar with white mold on it."

"Whoa - I don't know if you're ready for that," Forest yelled over the din. "That *mold* is opium. You up for big time hallucinations?"

There were a few silent glances back and forth between us, and a couple of anxious nods passed between Gina, Forest, the sorcerer, and me.

The sorcerer cut off about a six-inch chunk from the frosty slab and placed it on a scale. After he had recorded the weight in a little yellow book, he picked up the hash and double wrapped it in aluminum foil. (The price per gram was clearly marked on a large official chart hung up on the wall.) Then, as I pondered the absurdity of it all, I handed the money over to Forest who gave it to the sorcerer. Once we had the hash, the three of us scurried out of the Milky Way and glided arm in arm into the summer night and over to Forest's apartment.

We sat in breathless anticipation as Forest peeled back the foil. The chocolate hash gave us a little rush as the sweet biting aroma filled the space between us. We decided to give Gina the honors, and she rolled off a thick, soft wedge with her fingernail, molding it carefully into the tiny thimble-like bowl of a thin porcelain pipe. Forest struck a match, and we watched intently as Gina put the pipe to her lips.

"Take your time, rookie. Easy, easy," Forest cautioned. "Take it deep into your lungs, but don't take in too much or you'll cough it up."

Gina drew in deeply and purposefully. The opiate hash began to bubble and pop as it was drained slowly and evenly of its color and became a gray formless powder. Each of us performed the same rite, holding in the otherworldly smoke until it was absorbed into our lungs, and then we sat in silence and waited. Ever so slowly, I became aware that the room was vibrating with grotesque colors, and the air grew thick and fuzzy with ominus music.

Suddenly, everything took on a weird hypnotic glow. I found my feet and the three of us began dancing in a languid circle. Forest looked like a fearsome, blond-maned lion, and Gina like one of the intoxicated maenads painted on an ancient Greek vase. As we whirled around, I could feel my feet leave the ground. I felt as if I had no weight at all, as if I were an insubstantial and formless dark inertia, and when I let go of Gina's hand I seemed to merge into a melancholy painting of a decaying castle that was hanging on the wall. It was there in a dreary meadow surrounded by red-eyed satyrs and dying flowers that I fell under the spell of a black-robed demon.

When I opened my eyes it was morning, the sun was hopping across the golden-stained floor and I was glad to find myself lying in Gina's comforting arms. As Forest began serving freshly brewed coffee, I heard myself mutter, "Man, that chocolate hash is intense."

"You better go easy with that stuff," Forest replied with a knowing nod. "It'll burn out your brain."

"I still feel like I'm drifting in a dark daze," Gina added uneasily as she slid out from under me and went into a Yogic stretch.

Then, just as Forest was about to sit down, I heard my stomach rumble and yelled out, "Hey, guitar man, don't get too comfortable, we could use some grub."

"Yeah," Gina echoed, "I'm starving."

"How's ham and eggs?"

"Bring it on, Forest," I whooped.

After breakfast, we sat around rapping about art, philosophy, and politics, and singing along to Bob Dylan and Joni Mitchell records. Before we knew it afternoon had rolled around, and while we knocked off a few frothy beers and some funky sausages, Forest showed us some snapshots he had taken a few weeks earlier of Sitges, a tiny village on the coast of Spain, just south of Barcelona. As he stuffed them into a battered valise he added, "It's a very hip, laid-back scene with a lot of cool folks, mostly Euros, not too many Americans. If you've got the time you should go. I mean the place is really cool!"

As evening rolled around, we knew with that sixth sense travelers acquire that it was time to move on, and that Sitges was our next destination. We asked Forest to come along, but he said he had a real good paying gig coming up, one that he couldn't blow off. Gina was really disappointed, and before we split she made Forest swear he'd meet us in exactly one month at the entrance to the Coliseum in Rome.

INTERLUDE OF SHADOWS

Hast thou heard the secret counsel of God?
And dost thou limit wisdom to thyself?
What knowest thou, that we know not?
What understandest thou, which is not in us?

Book of Job

We flew into Barcelona about an hour ago and instantly fell in love with this ancient city of passion and tradition. Since I carried everything we needed in a lightweight backpack, we just wandered without a care from cafe to cafe, drinking golden beer and soaking in the local color.

It was just by chance that we stumbled into the Black Cat, a reconstruction of the original cafe that opened in 1897. While a jazz trio grooved away in the corner, we learned that the cafe was once a hangout of Picasso's and the site of his first show. When the trio took a break, I started up a conversation with the bass player whose name was Ricardo. Over a few malt whiskeys I learned about the Catalan people and their unique role and heritage in this region of Spain. When Ricardo found out we had just arrived, he insisted on taking us to a small hotel his father owned near the Gothic Quarter. We waited for him to finish his last set, and when it was over he guided us down a tree-lined street and into a small plaza.

We sat down next to a beautiful old fountain and Ricardo invited us to join him for some sangria. Soon that delightful fruity punch had us wagging our tongues about life in the States, and the appreciable difference between the relaxed pace in Barcelona and the mile-a-minute, materialistic lifestyle that passes for American culture. I was growing disconcertingly aware that not all people measured or defined themselves by the American standard. I had been born in the boom after World War II and had been showered with the great hopes and wealth of America. Along with millions of others, I had been nurtured in an educational incubator and taught that America was the land of opportunity for everyone, regardless of race, creed, or color. We were asked to believe in Freedom and Justice for All, and we did. We were given an American understanding of morality, of the world, and our place in it - which was at the top! We believed, truly believed, it was America's responsibility and our destiny to be the moral and political conscience of the world.

As long as we were kids, it really didn't matter, we could think or say anything we wanted. The problems began when the millions of us *kids* in colleges and universities all over America started to grow up and found our collective voice. We demanded that our parents, and our government, put into practice everything we had been taught. We had been asked to believe that America was good, just, noble, and honorable, and we really believed it. We wanted America to be all of that and more. But, while in college, we found out that our idealism and romantic views of life were the stuff of adolescent dreams: insubstantial and at odds with the entrenched social and political norms. In the wake of assassinations, unjust wars, and political and economic inequality, we rebelled and set out to devour the very system that brought us into being.

Of course, not everyone felt that way, but it was the fashionable thing to say that you did. I mean, our whole rebel life style - what we read, what we listened to, how we dressed - was in many ways more image than substance. We grew up spoiled and idealistic, expecting the world to give us everything we wanted. When you got right down to it, politics aside, it all boiled down to this: we wanted to live a life of love and freedom, and if you didn't like it - that was too damn bad!

Until I traveled to Europe, I had assumed that America, and American interests, were the center around which the world revolved. Now for the first time, I started to realize that American culture was loathed and blamed for most of the world's evils. But this understanding was soon lost as the sweet sangria took its hold and the plaza filled up with laughing people and strumming guitars.

We dined, drank, and danced under the stars, and as the evening drew to a close Ricardo led us up an ornate metal stairway and into a set of rooms his father had agreed to rent for the week. The three of us sat on the balcony, just content to chatter away and look out at the twinkling summer sky. When it began to grow late, Ricardo politely bid us goodnight. Soon the world around us grew still and we went inside. Then, with the stars gazing through the open doors of our balcony we tumbled into a thick, yielding mattress and into each other's arms. The delights of our bed were magical, and when the magic gave way to sleep I saw Gina and myself in a surreal dream.

It was a beautiful October day and we were back in the States, outside Philly, cruising in my Austin Healy convertible. We drove out to Bucks County, far away from the noise and babble of the city, following the back roads that curl through Holicong and Lumberville, taking us out of the hurly-burly and into the sweet fullness of grassy fields that lead to the High Rocks Overlook. We parked under an ancient oak and ran hand in hand through a kaleidoscope of orange and rust-colored leaves, running across a log bridge, intoxicated with sunshine and each other. Just below, a rough-hewn timber corral rose out of the shadows, its black outline set off against a plum-colored sky.

Through the tall grass, we could see two golden horses stirring up the dust, leaping from post to post, bucking and nipping at the air. Suddenly they stopped, and obeying an enchanted melody they alone could hear, began rubbing their majestic heads up, down, and across each other's golden-maned necks. Nestled in the tall grass just beyond the corral, we fell under the same spell and into each other's arms. Then, suddenly, it was late in the day, and the beech trees began shivering in the wind like solitary soldiers. Into the hills we climbed, followed by a cold sun that marched cross the pitted terrain, sending troops of shadows over moss-fringed rocks. We ambled across a swaying footbridge and, far below, the rocks rose up in defiance against the racing river pointing the way downstream through the bushes and thickening weeds. Up the stained incline we advanced, fighting our way through leafy shallows and over lifeless logs until, at last, we reached the top of a ruddy shale cliff where the wind carried us forward into space.

We're flying high above the world, devouring the air with god-like gulps, merging into the blueness, flying with the circling hawks over an immense horseshoe ravine, surrounded by a hundred thousand years of sap and sleep, bone and blood, immersed in a vast blueness of salutations and farewells, until the axis of convergence tilts and the still small orb of our being changes directions, spinning away from the infinite, taking us across continents and oceans, across the heavens and the star-filled skies until we're back once more in the embrace of Barcelona.

We've spent the past two days in our room fortified by sangria, the romantic strains of Spanish melodies, and fantastic flights of bliss. By day three, we resolved to get out of bed and gear up for an intense whirlwind tour of the city. I'm not sure how we did it, but in one dizzying weekend we took in the Picasso Museum, most of the Ramblas, and the churches of the Gothic Quarter.

CHURCHES. I had never seen so many churches. Although all of them were in some way magnificent and inspiring, I don't think I will ever forget the play of light through the centuries-old stained glass of the Cathedral of Barcelona. The shafts of light gave the fourteenth- and fifteenth-century wooden stalls a haunting, mystical quality which moved me profoundly.

Gina's favorite was the church of Santa Maria del Mar built in the mid-fourteenth century to honor the Virgin of the Sailors. We both marveled at the stunning rose window which bathed the vaulted columns in hues of translucent purity. Then again, you can only see so many churches before the whole scene gets a little old. After Santa Maria, we were ready to relax and just bask in the Spanish sun. Ricardo said he would hold our rooms, so we decided to take the afternoon train to Sitges.

We walked over to the station and as the train pulled in we both broke out in spasms of uncontrollable laughter. It was a scene right out of a Fellini movie: chickens, goats, and suckling babies, mixed together with a cast of gawking tourists, unflappable businessmen, squawking kids, garish prostitutes, and about fifty, black-clad matrons clutching their rosaries and praying intensely for deliverance. The train's windows were wide open, and the dirt, heat, and wind tossed newspapers and chickens up into the air creating glorious bedlam. Riding on that overcrowded train was a marvelous and exhilarating experience. In fact, I have rarely felt quite so alive as I did that day, smothered in the fecundity of Spanish flesh. Then, like an afterthought, we pulled into Sitges.

Gina and I maneuvered for the door and stepped out onto a narrow sandy street filled with ragtag kids, quizzical locals, and the delicious aroma of chicken and pork roasting over open fires. As we drew closer to the sea, the street widened a bit and led down to the beach and a large open-air bar. We decided to stop in for a drink, and found ourselves surrounded by an eccentric assortment of sandal-clad Europeans in bikini bathing suits and cut-off jeans, carousing in French, German, Dutch, and Spanish. Unexpectedly, I felt a hand on my shoulder, turned, and looked into the pleasant face of a longhaired guy, about my age, who spoke to me in English, but with a thick French accent. He introduced himself as André Rothschild, and around his neck was the biggest Star of David I had ever seen. When I told him I had been adopted by a Jewish family as an infant and raised as a Jew, he threw his arms round my neck and showered me with fraternal drunken kisses.

For the next twenty minutes, between shots of whiskey and cerveza chasers, André tried to make me understand the pervasive anti-Semitism he had experienced growing up in France. Then he asked me what it was like to be a Jew in America. Had I experienced the same sense of distrust? But before I had time to reply, he began shouting about the Germans and the Death Camps. Then, suddenly, he pointed an accusing finger around the bar and in a quivering voice yelled: "I spit on the lousy bastards! *They* knew . . . they all knew what Hitler and his gang were doing." Then, while shaking his head from side to side, he gestured upward crying, "God, where were You? Where were You when they threw us into the ovens?"

For a second, it seemed as if everyone had stopped talking. Then, with all eyes on him, André surveyed the bar, peered into my soul and whispered, "Where was God? Why did He give us up to our enemies?"

Everyone in the bar was really uptight; I could feel the bad vibes bouncing off us like a pulse of electromagnetic energy. Suddenly a paw-like hand covered in black hair grabbed the back of André's shirt. Amidst the shouting and scuffling, Gina managed to yank me by the arm and pulled me toward the door. As we made our exit, André ran passed us toward the train station, yelling and cursing, and shaking his fist toward the heavens. After looking for him for about an hour, we gave up and walked down to the beach.

The whole episode had really shaken me up. Although I was no longer very observant, I had grown up in a religious family, and what André said had really gotten to me. There was something chilling and compelling about his claim that "our enemies" - the Germans and all the other oppressors of the Jews throughout history - were still out to get us. Somewhere deep inside of me, André had touched upon a hidden fear, but thankfully, liquor and denial eventually made his ravings seem ludicrous, and my anxiety about being a Jew evaporated in the lingering summer sun.

Gina rested her head against my shoulder. As the warm wind blew up from the Mediterranean we walked slowly out onto a narrow strip of beach marked by jetties and brightly striped canvas cabanas. We checked into a small inn built up on the rocky shoal and were escorted to a spacious room which overlooked the darkening sea. The sky had turned a deep lavender, and from our balcony we could see directly below us a thin rope of colored lights suspended over a patio restaurant.

Later that evening we sat at a small candlelit table. Gina was dressed in a thin green sheath and the sea breeze caressed her dark, silky hair. The moon had risen full and lustrous, bathing the wooden fishing boats in deep silver shadows. The night air was alive with the song of seabirds and the deep resonant peal of harbor bells. At the suggestion of our waiter, we ordered a bottle of full-bodied Spanish wine and the seafood delight called paella. The paella was served to us on a large, handworked, silver plate overflowing with lobster, shrimp, squid, eel, and mollusk. The bounty was exquisite, masterfully arranged on a bed of simmering yellow rice, garnished with fragrant emerald herbs and slices of fiery red tomatoes. We ate this feast with abandon, prying out the steaming sea flesh with our fingers and licking the savory juices from our lips. We were drunk with food and wine and with each other.

As we stepped off the patio, we kicked off our sandals, and the sand felt cool and smooth under our feet. After walking about a quarter of a mile, the beach turned to the south. Within moments the town of Sitges disappeared, leaving us alone in a night of diamonds. The path we were following suddenly ended and before us stood a small, round, thatched-roof hut. We opened the screen door, went inside, took the smooth leather pad off the bench and placed it on the sand. Then everything grew very still as if the world had lost its voice. I think it must have been in that moment right before I sunk into a trance-like sleep that I heard an ancient voice calling out to me like a whisper on the wind:

> "Hear and Remember: The child must crawl before walking, and walk before running. This newborn child is Humankind, and your understanding of the Truth has been as the child who has crawled and walked, and now seeks to run.

> "In times past - in the East and the West - in places known to the many and in those known only to the few, in those faiths that are practiced and in those forgotten, the Prophets spoke to you with different words, but they all spoke the same Truth.

> "You are but many petals of the same renewing flower. Embrace, each of you, the one you call the Other and the Enemy: the Jew, the Christian,

the Muslim, the Hindu, the Buddhist, the Taoist, the Jain ... you are alike. For this world is of One Nature, One Character, and One God.

"In your infancy you were given the Word, each in your own time and place. Now recognize in your adolescence that your religions sound but one note. Look beyond those things by which you have made yourselves distinct and separate from each other.

"Know that these imagined differences are your cause of woe. They are inventions of the human mind fashioned by the customs of time and place wherein the Truth was revealed."

Then, inexplicably, I saw myself traveling backward across a sea of time to a previous life. I felt as if I were being swept away in a rushing, vibrant, shimmer of energy. It was so real I soon lost myself in the flush of forgotten sensations and dormant memories. Suddenly it was 1962, and, once again, I was back in Philly, hanging on the corner with the rest of the guys on a beautiful spring day.

I turned sixteen yesterday and that makes me six months older than Lenny Rothberg. Lenny's my best friend. He's stands six feet three inches tall and has pimples all over his face. He even has them on his massive belly which hangs out below his T-shirt like a grotesque, red-pitted balloon. Lenny is an oddity, but an oddity with incredible style. He's got a kind of fat kid's grace, an agility, a gift at winning the best-out-of-seven series in block baseball. Do you have any idea how good Lenny is? Bent over like a misshapen cactus he can cover an entire square of concrete on the sidewalk in front of Stan's candy store. With his enormous reach he can scoop up the lowest bouncer before it ever lands in the base-hit block. The boy is unbeatable! A superstar! A street corner legend!

Lenny's father is a kosher butcher and his mom's a music teacher. They live on top of the butcher shop. The store is kind of creepy with the dead chickens and cut up cow parts all over the place, but upstairs it's like a little museum with pictures everywhere. They even have a piano and long wooden shelves lined with hundreds of beautiful books. People think they're stuck up 'cause they got some money and a summerhouse in Long Beach Island. My father says they came to Philadelphia from Vienna and are "cultured." He says people are just jealous. They're pretty nice, once you get to know them. I'm the only kid from the corner they let in their house. I think it's 'cause I went to Hebrew School and the Rabbi once said in front of the whole congregation that I was the smartest kid in the school. They want Lenny to be a lawyer, and I bet he'll be one some day 'cause he's almost as smart as me.

Lenny's mom always treats me nice, so when I'm in their house I try to be very polite. Most of the time, to avoid getting the third degree, we hang out in his room and pretend we're doing homework or playing Scrabble while we sneak peeks at Playboy centerfolds. Lenny has these two older aunts - at least that's what he calls them. They're both real pretty, have long red hair, play the violin, and sleep in the same room. Lenny told me they walk around naked and sometimes even sleep together. I told him he was full of it, but he let me look through a tiny hole he made with a screwdriver in the wall that separates their bedrooms. Damn if he wasn't right! I got one good look and they were naked all right, and touching each other. I stopped when I heard someone coming up the stairs. I was afraid that it might be Lenny's dad. You don't want to mess with him. He's always coming up from the shop with knives in his hands and an apron smeared with blood.

Unless it's a weekend, Lenny's parents don't let him out of the house, except to go to school. They think all the kids on the corner are bad. They think we're gonna corrupt him. Well, it is kind of true, 'cause it seems whenever we're out on the corner the craziest things happen. Let me tell you what happened last Saturday. After a particularly sweaty, block baseball series, we hopped up on the hood of Ducky D'Amico's Dodge and polished off a few beers the Duck had hocked from his old lady's fridge, which the Duck did on a regular basis whenever his mom was making it with the ex-cop who lived next door. There we are, propped up on Ducky's Dodge, not giving a flying fart about anything, when from out of nowhere pulls up this real beat Yellow Cab. The door flies open and out struts this incredible young fox in the tightest pair of shorts I've ever seen. I mean she was really fine! Now I'm thinking to myself, *Who is this little peach with her tight black blouse and her tight white shorts?* when the cabby, all red-faced and ugly starts screaming, "Where you going, sister? You owe me five bucks, and you said your boyfriend was gonna pay up!"

Before I even know what I'm doing I got my wallet out and I'm digging up some cash, figuring that even if I don't get any real action she'd be worth five bucks just to fool around with. Besides, I made a fast ten off Chickie Roth the other night hustling nine ball at Mosconi's, so it really was no big deal. Anyway, I slide the cabby the ten, and while he's making change little Miss Peach sort of glides over to me rubbing herself against my leg. The next thing I know I got five bucks in my hand, the cabby's wheeling out, and me and Miss Peach got a date down by the trestle in the park at nine o'clock.

The first thing I did after Louise (that turned out to be Miss Peach's name) wriggled her way down the street and out of sight, was ask Ducky if he had a rubber. Well, that caused a real panic! The guys jumped in with their whistling and howling act, telling me "what for, 'cause you wouldn't know how to use it anyway," and putting me down with all the other jive talk corner boys make just to show how cool they are. Anyway, after all their ragging I discovered that nobody - not Ducky, not Lenny, not Chickie - nobody on the whole frigging corner even had a rubber. Then I somehow remembered, the way those people remember things when they wake up from getting hypnotized, that my father kept a pack of Trojans in his underwear drawer. I don't know how I knew that, but I did. It was just one of those weird things you know when you're a kid, even though you're not supposed to.

After dinner, when everybody's watching TV and things are kind of quiet, I sneak upstairs and start rooting around through my father's underwear. The whole time I'm thinking to myself, "Please God, let me find the old man's Trojans before he finds out what I'm doing." Then, just as I was ready to give up, I hit the mother lode: a box of Trojans and a fat tube of KY jelly. Ducky had told me all about the KY. He said if you put some on the tip of a rubber you could "get into anything." I grabbed a couple of Trojans, stuck the tube in my windbreaker, ran down the stairway, and flew out the front door.

The park was a short walk from the corner, and in it was a railroad bridge we called the Trestle. During the day you could watch and listen to the freight trains make their chick a boom music as they raced over the rails, and at night, if you were lucky, you might meet up with one of the Trestle girls who hung out there. If they were in the right mood, and if you had some beer and smokes, they just might put out for you. Tonight, I didn't need *no* luck and *no* Trestle girls, 'cause Louise would be waiting there just for me.

I can't remember why, but for some reason I told Lenny that I'd take him with me. I guess I felt sorry for him. He was a bit of a jerk, but he was always good for a couple of laughs. Anyway, before we head down to the park, we decide to catch a smoke on the corner and sing a little doo-wop with the guys from the Velvet-Tones. We jump right into Dion and the Belmonts, *Don't Know Why I Love You*. I take the falsetto, Lenny's comes in with the bass part, and my main man Chickie starts banging out the rhythm on the roof of Ducky's Dodge. Before we know it we're in a real groove and don't even realize that it's starting to get dark. When we finish up, Lenny runs into Stan's to cop a few stick matches off the soda fountain counter.

For an old guy, Stan was kind of weird; we could never figure him out. You might be sweating bullets, pinball machine propped on your toes, fifty points away from hitting, when Stan would finger pop one of those matches right in your face and blow your whole game. When Stan wasn't looking, Lenny grabbed a few sticks and we beat it out of there.

The Trestle was about half a mile into the park on the other side of the creek. As we walked through the grass the air smelled like spring and the pollen went to my head making me a little woozy. When we got near the creek, Lenny popped a couple of matches so we could scope out the situation. The only way to get to the other side was to balance yourself on the rocks that peeked out over the water. I had made this crossing a hundred times, but never at night with the biggest kid in the neighborhood hanging onto my belt loops.

"C'mon Lenny," I yell. "Move that fat butt. Step on that rock, the big one, not the one covered with frog slime."

Somehow we're jumping from rock to rock. Lenny's pulling on my belt loops and we're flying over those rocks. Then on the other side, sprawled out and wet up to the knees, I throw a headlock on the goofy dork. I smack him upside the head a few times and we start wrestling and laughing like donkeys.

After we catch our breath, I pull out this flask of whiskey Cochise laid on us earlier that day. I had taken a few sips of whiskey a couple of times from my Dad's liquor cabinet and nothing much happened, but Cochise said *this* was the good stuff, 150 proof, and would really get us flying. With a name like Cochise you'd have thought he was an Indian, but he was really an Irish ex-cop named Mick Regan. In fact, he was the guy who was always banging Ducky's mom. Mick got his nickname after he cut up this wise guy in a knife fight. He was so good with the blade that the corner boys named him Cochise after that Indian guy on television.

As we head down the path to the Trestle, Lenny takes a big gulp from the flask and rolls his eyes as he passes it over. My first swig burns all the way down to my belly, but after a few more the burning stops and I feel like I'm walking in a warm sweet fog. Up ahead I see Louise swaying under a big tree and in an instant I'm pressing hard against her. She grabs the flask from my hand, starts sucking it down, and soon we're locked in a hot whiskey kiss. After a while the stars start popping like flashbulbs in my head and I know I'm getting real high. Then kind of low and sweet, like a little songbird, I hear Louise calling for her girlfriend Pam who's standing in the shadows. I call Lenny over, and now the four of us are drinking and smooching. A couple of minutes later, Lenny and Pam drift off behind a bush and start shuffling and moaning. That's when I take one more long swig and watch as Louise licks the last few drops of whiskey off the flask with the tip of her tongue.

Suddenly, we fall to the ground and really start making it. We're frenching, and as my hand goes under her bra I'm telling Louise how fine she is, that she's beautiful, that I love her, and anything else I can think of. My hands find their way across her little behind, down the back of her shorts and over her smooth soft legs. It feels like her whole body is enveloped in an electrified fluid. I can feel the silk fuzz on her thighs brush against me, and as I lick the honeysuckle off her neck she starts making love noises in my ear. Now I'm pulling at her shorts, and her panties slide down around her ankles. Her hands are all over me and I'm free. I'm swinging big and thick, flying by instinct and radar. Then we're on the ground and I'm inside her. I'm inside for the very first time, and it's slick and creamy. The colors of the universe are exploding in my head and there ain't no time for Trojans and KY jelly.

Now she's on top of me, first moving real slow and then real fast. She's sliding up and down on me like I'm a barber pole, and I can't tell anymore if I'm inside her or she's inside me. I don't know what's happening, but I'm praying to God so I won't come. I'm thinking about playing block baseball, and hanging out on the corner, and singing doo-wop, and the time Lenny and me had a fight and my eye was blood red for a week. I'm thinking about everything except doing it. Then, somehow, I'm not sixteen anymore, I'm not with Louise, and I'm not in Philly. I'm back in Sitges and the past and present have converged. I'm holding Gina so tightly I can hardly breathe; holding on to my exposed dreams, my ghosts, my demons. Holding on tightly as we ride a wave of erotic music, turning each other inside out, spinning in a whirlpool of sap and steam. Nothing else matters, nothing else exists but the pushing and pulling, the choking saliva, and the divine light at the bottom of the ocean. Nothing else remains, yet through the nothingness the eternal rhythm is felt in every cell: chick a boom, chick a boom, chick a boom, boom, boom.

Around mid-morning, we were jolted out of our erotic reverie by two, pig-tailed, freckle-faced imps who were showering us with a bucket of sand and seawater. Gina jumped up from the makeshift bed with murder in her eyes, but when she saw how dumbfounded and ridiculous I looked, she started laughing. Well that set me off and we both began howling. After a couple of minutes we got it together, wiped each other off, and put our clothes back on. We emerged from the thatched-roof hut with our dignity in tact, and as we walked back to our hotel gave a thumbs-up to the bemused sunbathers and their children.

The next few days in Sitges were filled with the soothing sound of the Mediterranean Sea washing up on the golden sand. Yet during that entire time, I kept replaying that scene in the bar with André Rothschild, thinking about what he said about the Germans, and how they were *still* out to get the Jews. With our return to Barcelona came the realization that I had to find out if he was right.

We had planned to go to Switzerland after leaving Spain, but with a little loving persuasion Gina agreed to fly first to Germany. We spent our last day hanging out with Ricardo, promising to write, and to return one day to Barcelona. It was with a sincere and lingering regret that we slowly boarded the plane that would take us to Munich, the city where Hitler first came to power.

The flight from Barcelona to Munich was uneventful and routine, but the moment we touched down at the Franz Josef Airport I was gripped by an oppressive anxiety. As I got off the plane, I felt as if everyone was looking at me and wondering if I were a Jew. A generation ago I would have been furnace fodder, and now I was just another happy American tourist visiting the land of suds and swastikas.

I had heard that Munich was a real party town, overflowing with rosy-cheeked frauleins and Bavarian beer gardens. I tried to keep that in mind as we waited in line to go through Customs. Much to my dismay, we had to pass by a thick-jawed, impassive Customs Officer dressed in a stiff, gray, military-like uniform. As I handed over my passport, he studied it carefully, squinting at my name and my face. When he glanced up his eyes were menacing little slits, and it seemed to me that he enjoyed stamping my passport with the official German seal. As he returned my papers and motioned to me to step across the yellow line, I thought I heard him whisper, "Jude." With that one word I felt for the first time what it meant to live in fear, to have your life placed in the hands of strangers who hated you and thought nothing of killing you and your kind. I knew this was a morbid fantasy and that nothing like this was really happening, but my heart was pounding as we boarded the bus that would take us from the airport to Munich's downtown terminal.

I guess I appeared agitated because Gina asked me if anything was wrong. I told her that I had an upset stomach, and she suggested that I take a nap, adding cheerily that she'd wake me up when we arrived in Munich. As I shut my eyes I shuddered and tried to remember that Munich was the site of the Oktoberfest. I tried to visualize thousands of jolly Germans dancing merrily and guzzling pitchers of beer, but instead I saw thousands of emaciated Jews at the Dachau concentration camp built by the Nazis on the outskirts of Munich in 1933. I shuddered again and found myself, not in Dachau, but in the small, sanctified chapel at the back of the synagogue I went to every Sunday morning as a boy of twelve.

There are about fifteen of us training for our Bar Mitzvahs, learning how to perform the ritual of putting on phylacteries - two, small, square wooden boxes, bound in shiny black leather, containing slips inscribed with scriptural passages. Attached to each box is a set of long black leather straps. There's a special way you have to tie them, one around your left hand and arm, the other across your forehead.

Huddled underneath a cascading linen prayer shawl, I tightened the leather straps. The phylacteries cut into my flesh, each leather strip branding me as a Jew. Then together, in one shrill voice, we began our chant, bobbing and bowing towards the Torah Scrolls partially revealed behind the gold-embossed curtain of the Ark. As we sang the plaintive Hebrew prayers of the Morning Service, we thanked God for renewing us with life in His miracle of Creation. Yet, as we sang out the *Shema* - extolling God's glory and Oneness, and vowing to remain faithful to the way of our fathers - I couldn't help wondering what it really meant to be this thing called a Jew, and why some of the kids I played with on my block were allowed to eat that mouth-watering bacon, and why their houses had beautiful pictures of Mary and Jesus on their living room walls. Why, I wondered, were these things forbidden to me? What was it that made me different from all those other kids?

Sometimes, even in the midst of earnest prayer, when my little soul was filled with fervor and genuine awe, I just couldn't help thinking about Willie Mays and the Giants playing the Phillies at Connie Mack Stadium, and the time Joey Finkle pulled down Shelly Greenbaum's tube top on the Hebrew School steps, and how Shelly gasped and struggled, but made sure we all saw her boobs before she pulled the top back up.

I knew it was wrong to think about such things. I tried not to, praying even harder, tugging fiercely at the black leather straps winding down from my elbow to my fingers. Yet, when I looked around at all the other boys caught up in the soaring sounds of our cracking voices, I couldn't help but wonder what we were all really doing here, and how I got to be a Jew, and why I was performing this ancient ritual instead of lying on the living-room floor watching TV and reading the Sunday comics.

After services, Mrs. Popkin would give us hot chocolate with our bagels and lox in the little room behind the chapel. In some ways, this was another deep and puzzling mystery. I'd ask myself, *How was it possible that Mrs. Popkin who looked so hideous with her matted hair, sweaty face, pink warts, and coarse, white chin hairs could be so gentle and kind?* When she poured the hot chocolate, she tried to conceal a string of tiny numbers that peeked out from under the sleeve of her ratty sweater.

It seemed to me that for Mrs. Popkin this trail of bluish lines was the visible reminder of some terrible secret burned into her flesh and soul by the finger of God. I wondered if it were possible to decipher that secret code and, by doing so, set her free from the torment and sorrow set into her eyes like a dim, cold, eternal light. Yet, even as I struggled to understand the meaning of the mysterious and terrifying inscription that stretched out like a broken bridge over swollen veins and scab-covered skin, I found myself tottering on the edge of revulsion. For although Mrs. Popkin always spoke with gentle kindness, when she bent down hovering an inch from my face her breath was as foul-smelling as sewer stench. Ashamed and bewildered, I turned away. I hated her, and hated that part of me that was like her. But there was no escape from Mrs. Popkin, just as there was no escape from myself. I shuddered as I looked down at the numbers on her arm and wondered if one day God would place his mark on me.

At that moment, my only wish was that Mrs. Popkin would die - not really die - but just move away, move down the table, move back into the kitchen. Then she looked at me oddly, as if I reminded her of someone else, perhaps some other child she had once pressed to her black shrouded breast. Maybe that was the secret of the numbers. Each one stood for a child, a child just like me, a lost child for all the old Jewish women who walked across the tear-stained earth.

I knew Mrs. Popkin really couldn't understand what I was thinking or why I was so upset, but I thought she wanted to understand. I'm not even sure I understood what my thoughts really meant, or what was happening to us. Yes, to us! For we seemed bound by an invisible, spiritual energy, as if we had merged together into a new soul, a brave soul, a soul strong enough to stare into the face of evil. Mrs. Popkin stood over me like an immovable mountain, a protective unflinching power, and I saw that the dim light in her eyes had become a spark of fire. And that spark of fire filled the hollow of my heart with a rapture I had never known. It was then, in that evanescent moment of bliss, I saw a face as familiar as my own rise up before my eyes and heard an astonishingly beautiful voice singing in my soul like a hymn coming from beyond the stars:

> "Throw down your weapons and embrace the call to Love. Celebrate Goodness, Righteousness, and Peace, and you will come to believe in the simplicity of the first truth: I am God and You are with Me.

> "Speak the Words you have heard in your Inner-Being into the ears of all you meet, and the Truth will not go unheard. Remember that those who are given the most are those who must do the most."

Then, somehow, the wondrous, indescribable voice in my soul and Mrs. Popkin's voice became one, and I heard Mrs. Popkin whisper with a depth of love I shall never forget, "Eat my child, have chocolate. No, no, do not worry, God will not forsaken you."

Suddenly, the bus jerked violently and I tumbled out of my vision. I was no longer a boy of twelve lost in prayer - I was

41

in Munich - and absolutely certain that coming here was a big mistake. As I climbed out of my seat, I got this sinking feeling in my stomach that shot up into my head. I leaned dizzily against an armrest, and as Gina wrestled the backpack off the overhead rack I turned to catch it as it fell sideways into my arms. I tumbled out of the bus behind her, and though I could see her lips moving and could distinguish a word or two, I couldn't really make out what she was saying. My mind went woozy, and as I lamely followed her, the world around me became a slow-motion movie.

When we stopped walking, I found myself in a great square surrounded by shops, cafes, and outdoor restaurants. Gina was pointing at a very tall, white column. I looked over her outstretched arm, and high above was a beautifully rendered statue.

"Isn't she beautiful," Gina said devoutly. "That's the Holy Mother of God."

My head was still spinning as I heard her say that we were in the Marienplatz, the heart of Munich, and that the statue high above our heads was the Virgin Mary. At that moment, I had this macabre vision of Hitler, nonchalantly sipping a beer underneath the soaring image of the Holy Mother while plotting out the Final Solution to the Jewish Problem. Under the pretext of needing something to eat, I hustled Gina over to the nearest cafe and flopped down at a heavy, dark, wooden table. Shaking in a fog of irrational fear, I spent the next hour drinking beer with a crowd of singing Bavarians and picking halfheartedly at Schweinshaxe, which I learned from a strapping waiter who looked like the archetypal Hitler youth, was pickled pork knuckle.

Gina had pulled out our guidebook and was circling hotel addresses when I blurted out that I was feeling ill from the pork knuckle, which I really was. Then I added, with as much bravado as I could muster, that I wanted to return to the terminal and take the first train to Zurich. Gina gave me an incredulous stare, and then, as if she had just gotten the joke, started laughing.

"Oh, I see. You dragged me to Germany from Spain, when I wanted to go to Switzerland in the first place, and now you want to leave after we've just gotten off the plane, bused into town, and sat down to lunch." She pursed her lips, paused for a moment, and said, "Did I get it right, Jonny?"

I wanted to tell her how I felt about the Germans and the Jews, but I just couldn't. Instead I kept blathering that I was sick, that I needed to get some fresh air, needed to go to Switzerland, needed to go up into the Alps. I guess Gina knew I was desperate, because after a few more frantic pleas she caved in and I hailed the first taxi I saw. We jumped in the back and were at the train station in minutes. Owing to luck, or a bit of divine intervention, the evening train to Zurich was just arriving. In fact, the second I finished purchasing our tickets it pulled in. Hurriedly I climbed onboard; Gina followed, hesitantly.

As we entered our compartment and the train began to pull away from the terminal, I felt a sense of relief bordering on elation. If at that very second it would have been possible, I'd have found the phylacteries of my youth, bound myself in those leather straps, and standing in the open window of the railway car for all Germany to see, thanked God for delivering me from my enemies.

Within minutes, I returned to my old charming self and managed to convince Gina we had done the right thing, without telling her the real reason I wanted to leave Germany. I probably should have come clean and told her exactly what I was going through. But as close as we were, I was afraid that she wouldn't understand my terror and fear of the Holocaust. No, that was something only other Jews could really understand. Besides, we had gotten out of Germany, and that was all that really mattered.

We arrived in Zurich the next day without mishap, and, after checking in at the extraordinarily posh and genteel Baur au Lac Hotel, decided to hit the streets. Even though Zurich is the largest city in Switzerland, it's very foot-friendly. In fact, it feels as if you could take in the whole town in one day.

All of the travel books tell you to begin with a stroll past the world-famous jewelry shops where everything is set into eighteen-carat gold - so that's what we did. From there, we headed south and then east over to Zurich's oldest church which has the distinction of having the largest clock-face in Europe. (Speaking of clocks, watches, and every other kind of timepiece, they're everywhere you look. One can easily understand why the Swiss are extremely punctual; it's part of their national character.) After that, we crossed the Limmatt River and meandered over to the oldest section of the city which is like stepping back into medieval times. The cobblestone streets and narrow lanes date back to the twelfth century, and all the buildings have been marvelously preserved.

The next day we rose early and took the bus from Zurich to Bern, passing through towns and villages of immaculate cleanliness and order. The gingerbread houses looked as if they had popped out of a children's book of fairy tales. The entire country was a giant health spa, dripping in Technicolor valleys and lakes.

I don't think I have ever felt quite as invigorated as I did during our short stay in Switzerland. Everyone and everything effused an aura of good health. The old men walking their dogs looked as if they could win triathlons; the children were Heidi clones; the women, pumped up with goat's milk and yogurt, made Playboy centerfolds look underdeveloped. And the air! How can I describe the air of Switzerland? It's as if you're breathing the essence of the planet, becoming aware for the very first time that this life-giving force, which we draw in without a thought, is the product of a natural order to which we have become desensitized. With every breath, you realize that each one of us is connected to and a part of the flow of things in a way so elegant and sublime that it almost eludes perception.

In Switzerland, I became intuitively aware that I was created by the union of the sun and earth, of the sea and sky. I was the transmutation of the elements. With an unaccustomed clarity of thought, I realized what the Holy men of the East really meant when they said they did not need food and could live on air alone, and in this exalted state could glimpse Nirvana. Such was my frame of mind as we pulled into the bus station in Bern and hopped a tram to nearby Lake Thun. We checked into a quiet alpine lodge and spent the remainder of the day walking lazily along the edge of the lake. The late afternoon sun brought the outline of dozens of white swans into bold relief as they glided effortlessly over the tranquilizing blueness. As we began the long walk back to the lodge, I began thinking about the trip we were taking to Grindelwald, and tried to imagine how I would feel standing amidst the clouds at the top of the world.

Back at our hotel, we had a light dinner and turned in for the night, but before I fell asleep I felt a twinge of anticipation at the promise the morning's adventure held. Then as the goats bleated and the frogs croaked, I fell into a deep and enduring slumber.

I awoke the next morning groggy and confused, sunk in disturbing dreams of Dachau. But as the sun peeked through the curtains and flittered across the floor the troubling nightmares vanished. By 7:00 a.m., we had breakfasted on coffee, yogurt, and pastries; half an hour later, we boarded the train to Grindelwald. As it fought its way upward through mist-filled valleys and soaring hillsides, we leaned against the half-open windows awestruck by the grandeur of the rising peaks. It was just like the scene in that classic, black and white Ronald Coleman movie, where the camera draws back and gives the audience its first enticing glimpse of Shangri-La. Right in front of us stood the mythical realm of immortality, not the celluloid fantasy. No, this was the real thing, ablaze in color, sound, and fury.

The train climbed higher and higher, until a thick mountain fog swallowed it up. It reappeared momentarily in the face of a blazing sun before plunging into a black tunnel of rock and ice. A few minutes passed before the train emerged and came to a halt at the center of the Jungfrau, a ring of snow-capped mountains floating in a sea of luminous clouds. The only way to proceed to Grindelwald was to disembark and board a tiny rectangular passenger car that hung on a black cable. The cable was connected to a series of short towers that seemed to sprout out of the mountainside every hundred yards.

We entered the car short of breath and full of anxiety. Somewhere, high above us, we heard the whir of motors. The monorail lurched forward and upward at a sixty-degree angle, defying common sense and gravity. Gina and I clung to each other as the car swayed back and forth on its ascent into space. Without warning, the observation deck, a tiny sliver of wood and iron sticking absurdly out of the mountain wall just below the crown, appeared right above us. The winch and the car came to an abrupt halt; cautiously, we stepped out onto the observation platform.

How can I describe the ineffable power of the vision we beheld? It was the grandeur of God flying on the clouds, laughing joyously throughout the universe. And in the sound of the laughter, I thought I heard a Cosmic Voice singing in my soul, reawakening a distant memory:

> "The moment of Creation is one burst of Light. The Truth, like the Light, is unchanging and the same through all Time. What you believe to be different truths are but reflections of the unchanging Truth and the eternal Word.
>
> "Bring together the religions of the world and embrace their beauty, for they are reflections of the same Truth.
>
> Cherish the way in which the Truth is heard. Though it may sound different, the Truth is like many different voices singing the same note."

At that moment, I too, wanted to sing. But as the miraculous vision began to fade from my mind, all I could do was surrender to the awesome mystery and the jubilant voice that filled every aspect of my being.

Two days after we returned from Grindelwald, right before sunrise, we boarded the train to France. Maybe it's due to lack of sleep (I've been plagued by terrifying nightmares of the Dachau concentration camp since we left Germany), but I just don't feel like myself anymore, and I found the first part of the 250-mile trip from Switzerland to the French Riviera acutely disturbing. My irritability factor was really high, and though I tried not to jump down Gina's throat every time she said something, I wasn't very successful.

"Jonny, what's your problem?" Gina said with a rising annoyance. "All I asked was if you wanted some coffee!"

"If I want coffee, I'll get it myself. I don't need any help from you!"

With that, Gina marched off in a huff. I don't know what's wrong with me, maybe my nerves are shot, but I was in such a shitty mood that I didn't even try to stop her. (She returned about ten minutes ago, without the coffee, plopped down next to me, and hasn't uttered a word.)

We're traveling to the seaside city of Nice, partly as a whim, and partly because a lovely older couple told us that it was their favorite Mediterranean vacation spot. Even though the train is supposed to pass through some panoramic countryside as it hugs the coast, I've decided to hunker down into the soft, deep, leather-cushioned seat and try to grab a few Z's.

When I opened my eyes the sun was high in the sky, and we were pulling into the train station at Nice. I felt washed out and edgy, just itching for a good fight. (I know I must've had another evil dream, even though I can't remember a damn thing.)

Fortunately, Gina's mood had changed, and she was feeling chipper enough for the both of us. It was all "bon jour" as we climbed off the train. The station was a flurry of excitement done up in gay pastels, smelling of flowers and fresh-baked bread. I could feel my spirits rising as a fleet of railroad attendants sporting Maurice Chevalier mustaches and wearing uniforms of cheery light blue accented by pink boutonnieres greeted us.

Gina's French was very good. Within minutes she had directions to the Beau Rivage, a small hotel made famous by Matisse who had painted the *Open Window* while lodging there in 1917. I felt almost light-hearted as we casually strolled up the Boulevard of the Angels toward the hotel. It was lunchtime, and people poured out into the street with the kind of joyous vitality that typifies life on the Riviera.

Within minutes we had checked into the hotel. As we were led into a trendy, art nouveau room awash with sunshine and overlooking the sea, I felt as if I had stepped into Matisse's painting. Out on a small, black metal balcony, just as in the *Open Window*, were three terra cotta flowerpots arranged in a neat row, set off by pale green walls that were mirrored in uneven glass panes reflecting the pink and blue tints of the sky. Just out of reach, in a soft spread of aquamarine, were the same rust-colored furled sails and the mauve-tinged masts of the wooden fishing boats.

Wistfully, I turned away from the window and saw Gina lying on the tiny bed like a flower on a spread of white cloth. As I watched her resting so peacefully, it seemed as if I were bathing in a warm wave of healing light and Gina was the center of this emanating flow. As I snuggled beside her, right before I drifted off to sleep, I was gripped by an intense unshakable intuition: I knew Gina would love when others would condemn, find pity when others would seek retribution, and suffer in her frailty so that I might find the strength to forgive. I knew that I would be the cause of her sorrow with a certainty based not on fact or reflection, but as an undeniable truth at the core of my being. Yet I knew these solemn truths only as things that one knows in misty dreams and visions that disappear from memory with the advance of the morning sun.

The next morning we rose at dawn, and while breakfasting on croissants and coffee reviewed our itinerary. In exactly twelve days, we were going to meet Forest at the entrance to the Roman Coliseum. With almost two weeks to kill, we decided to spend at least a few days just drinking in sunshine and wine, then proceed by train to Florence for an intense Renaissance culture fix, and then south to Rome. (I had read that the Eternal City was ungodly hot in August, but Gina wanted to visit the Vatican, we both wanted to see Michelangelo's achievement in the Sistine Chapel, and, of course, there was our long-awaited reunion with Forest.)

After breakfast, we put on a couple of skimpy bathing suits and sauntered out to the beach. Actually, the beach at Nice could hardly be described as a beach at all, unless you included in the definition, a uniform spread of unattractive, hand-size, gray flat rocks scattered over a coarse brown bed of sand. I was amazed at the way people would spread a thin towel across the rocks and catch a few rays. After a tall glass of champagne I tried it myself. Surprisingly, it wasn't quite as uncomfortable as it looked. Still, Gina and I both opted for low-slung canvas chaises that you could rent by the day. Supported by fresh fruit, wine, and covered with Ban de Soleil, we whiled away the afternoons, and in the evenings indulged in the finest cuisine money could buy.

Well, we spent almost a week in this state of high living, and although I still had a few grand in traveler's checks, Gina picked up the tab for the whole jaunt. At first, I had some misgivings about being a moocher, but it sure was nice going first-class. Anyway, since today was our last day on the French Riviera, I decided that I wasn't going to let anything bother me - especially guilty feelings about spending Gina's money.

As sort of a parting gesture of decadence, we took a few hits of the Amsterdam hash before heading down to the beach, and man did we get wasted. We spent most of the day sunbathing in a warm, caressing wind, and when I finally came down I wrote this bizarre poem on the inside cover of my guidebook.

HIGH UP TO DOWN LOW

Thinly tapered palm trees arch upward,
Painlessly capturing day's fleeting light.
Gnarled tree trunks jut downward,
Fanning clay tents aloof from history.

Humming engines parade backward,
Suffocating sidewalks of heat-beat summer.
Purple dust moralists wheeze forward,
Zonking lemon trees with chromium fire.

Depressed mermaids ravage young sailors,
Pacing proudly in silk print dresses.
Pink-lipped babies cry and suck,
Assassinating bread-begging mothers.

Chinese fat cats eat American cheese,
Tunneling westward to Washington.
Pimps with whips dance eastward,
Swallowing golden-coated oil wells.

On the beach, on the beach,
The circus has begun.
Sanguine harlots hump and bump,
And the tent comes falling down.

When I read the poem to Gina the strangest thing happened.
The moment I finished, she whipped off her bikini top and began
whirling it round her head. Then she kissed me hotly, called me a
pimp, and with an impish laugh ran into the sea.

SYNCHRONOUS CODA

When the people of the world
all know beauty as beauty;
Then arises the recognition of ugliness.
When they all know the good as good;
There arises the recognition of evil.

Way of Lao Tzu

We arrived in Florence a few days ago and are staying in a little hotel near the Uffizi Gallery. We've gone there every day, but even with all its wonders something is very wrong.

I've been up most of the night drinking wine and smoking hash, and I feel as if I'm sinking into a dark fever. Lately, all I want to do is smoke the stuff. It's a craving, a hunger that I need to feed. I'm afraid it's killing me, eating away my soul and destroying my mind, leaving only a void of searing pain hot enough to burn through steel and alien supermetals.

I've gone two nights with hardly any sleep. There's a ringing in my ears and an ache in my left shoulder that won't go away. My mind is filled with vile and malignant thoughts, and I'm afraid something very bad is going to happen. Something inside of me at the very center of my being that was once whole is coming undone. Whatever it is that I am is unraveling like a long fine thread carried away on the wind.

I haven't written a word in days, not one single word since I scribbled that bizarre poem on the beach at Nice. I may never write again for with the words come more lies. How do I get beyond the lies? How do I avoid getting lost in the words, in their superfluity and endless combination? What do these allusions, metaphors, and evocation of feelings that push pen across paper really mean? If I could write just one truthful sentence I think all the illusions would dissolve and humankind would be born anew. I want to get beyond the artifice and appearance of things. I want to get beyond the words and live in the Truth. This, I believe, was the gift of Jesus to humankind. He alone, with total belief, became the Embodiment of Truth, and showed us how to live as the Son of God.

Gina is asleep beside me, and through the outlined vee of linen sheets I can feel her heat summoning me. I want to lift the shroud that separates us, unearth the twisted root and drown in the alchemist's draught, but I am immobile, and even the sweetest fruit cannot bring me back to life. Just now I thought I heard the call of a strange but familiar voice. From deep within it said: "Join me, and we will gaze fearlessly into the mouth of Moloch. Join me, and you will see the swirling cauldron of protein and biochemical ooze which flows through beast and bee. Drink, drink, and for you this night of sleeplessness will end." And so I drank deeply and shamelessly, and the words poured out like blood from an open wound.

GANYMEDE

In his eyes I saw the promise of love.

What promise did he see in me,
Staring at him hungrily
Through the open windows
Of the farm workers' bus?

Today, on the Fourth of July,
Where was he bound?
Where was this dark-haired, dark-eyed,
Beautiful boy bound?

Whose faces are trembling in the shadows?
Mother? Father? Sister? Brother?
How they huddle in their speeding tomb.

Look at his eyes.
What is that light,
That light of soul that shines so brightly?

How I ache for that sweet child.
I would eat of his flesh, drink of his lips,
Rejoice in his translucent beauty.

Like Zeus, I will reach down and seize him.

He will become a gull, a dolphin, an angel,
And know the ocean is his father,
And the earth his mother.

Child of Light, do not be afraid.
I am not the demon of your dreams;
I am not the beast in the shadows.

I am the crashing wave dancing in the sun.
I am the lichen and the seaweed,
And the stars spinning in the night.

Today, on this Day of Independence,
I will pluck the thorns, kiss your wounds,
And deliver you from your daily crucifixion.

No, do not cry and dim those eyes.
I will call to you like a whisper on the wind.
A whisper on the wind is all that I am,
And all that I am is my sweet Ganymede.

Gina awoke about 10:00 a.m., we drank some wine and tried to get it on, but nothing happened. We went at it for about ten minutes, but it just wouldn't work. We blamed each other and it got mean and nasty. Gina went downstairs about a half an hour ago to get some breakfast and to think things over. No, things are not going well. We're no longer alive in our love, merely going through the motions, filling up the hours with diversion and amusement, smiling our way through the empty days. Maybe this is our swan song, full of melancholy and bitter tears. I feel played out, older than the Biblical scenes exquisitely frozen in bronze on the Baptistery doors. There's a sickness consuming my soul and a growing revulsion for everything that is good and beautiful. In fact, the whole Florentine art scene with its grace and harmony is making me sick. I swear, yesterday in the Uffizi, I almost lost my lunch. Too much harmony, too much grace, too much Genius!

About twenty minutes ago Gina came back to the room. We were on the verge of killing each other until I went out and scored some tabs of Valium. We each dropped a few, and now we're as mellow as neutered pussycats dozing in the sun. After a long, leisurely lunch, we began an excessively polite discussion of *The Dwarf*, a remarkable little book. I really got caught up in the little bastard's antics and torments, in his loathing and hatred of humanity. The ideals of the Renaissance, when seen through the unflinching eyes of the court misfit, become contemptible. In the dwarf's worldview we are a greedy, spiteful, and corrupt lot, and what passes for genius is an oddity.

Now I finally understand: the story of the dwarf is my story! It is the story of every man who has been marked as an outcast, for we are a freakish brood surviving only by good fortune and chicanery. It is this realization, this balancing act of an elephant on a pin, that forces me to reexamine my little meanderings, my bashes at poetry, and dives into self-pity and indulgence. Now, for the first time, I see what a ridiculous and absurd fellow I really am.

Can you imagine my embarrassment? Everywhere I have gone, I have been looking for meaning and for answers. Everywhere I have been, underlying all the frantic hedonism and purging of the senses, I heard myself asking, *Who's in control?*

Now, in a flash, everything has become so clear and obvious: No one's in control, and I am the only one who can give my life meaning. Just to be alive, just to be here with Gina in Florence - even in this moment of exquisite angst - is a most wonderful gift. Much to my astonishment, I realize that I have been a fool and forgotten how to laugh. So now I laugh as we walk through churches, galleries, and museums. I laugh under the stares of sanctimony, authority, and conventionality. I laugh at all the dead dukes and kings, bishops and popes, mad men and saints. I laugh at the painters, the sculptors, and the philosophers with their inflated ideas about youth, beauty, and love. I laugh myself right into existence and know that it is my laughter that keeps me alive. I laugh until the sound is louder than the voices in my head and the ringing in my ears, louder than thunder, louder than the great, unheard Big Bang. Like Adam, I too have been expulsed from the Garden, but I am not ashamed of my nakedness. I have taken my hands away from my eyes and beheld a world of dizzying wonder and possibility. God has given me the power of understanding and said, "Go forth and learn what it is to be a man."

We rolled into Rome exactly three days ago, checked our baggage at the train station and went out on the town. Gina's dolled up in black leather and I'm wearing this buckskin fringed vest and purple cowboy boots. We're on a bender, that's for sure. We've already worked our way through nine or ten trendy clubs on the Via Luciani.

Just for a few laughs, I've been throwing some money around, telling bartenders I'm Gina's manager, and that she just recorded an album with the Stones. I guess the bartenders must have tipped off the paparazzi, because they're following us around like were rock stars! When Gina hiked up her skirt on the dance floor, they went wild. Just for the hell of it, I smacked one of them when he tried to crawl between her legs and take a picture.

After that little scene, I must have blown a couple of hundred bucks buying everyone drinks as a gesture of reconciliation. That extravagance has given a zest and truthfulness to our "Last Escapade." That's what Gina's been calling everything that's happened to us since I smacked the photographer. Now, everywhere we go, like a scene out of *La Dolce Vita*, the whole pack follows us on sleek, red motor scooters. An exceptionally garish transvestite who goes by the name of Lorena guides us from club to club, and as we weave down the cobblestone streets, Gina calls out, "Join us on our Last Escapade!" as if she expects the world to come crashing down at any moment.

Early this morning, I lit up a fat wedge of the Amsterdam hash in one of the underground clubs and turned on about a dozen of our following. I was so liquored up that I barely felt the hashish coming over me. When it hit, I grabbed hold of Gina and pulled her onto the floor. Right after that, Lorena and an ebony-skinned transvestite named Claudia stripped down to lingerie, and in the glare of chintzy, mirrored walls took on two macho types wearing nothing but black leather jock-straps. Half-cocked against a thick padded wall, Gina and I watched the kinky show play out.

It must have been about eight in the morning when our little troupe emerged from the underground and slithered onto the freshly washed, sun-streaked street. Like vampires after a feed, we hung inside the safety of the dark rising shadows. Then with murmured good-byes and averted stares, Gina and I scurried towards the Coliseum. We spent the morning drinking espresso in a bleak little cafe. After a few jolts, the pasty, wiped-out face that stared back at me in the mirror above the lunch counter once more became someone that I knew. As we went over our plans for our meeting with Forest, I watched Gina undergo the same humanizing transformation.

We arrived at the Coliseum about a half an hour before noon. The sun had climbed overhead, and as I looked out over the imposing stadium, I shielded my eyes from the glare that bounced off the maze of stone passageways and arches. The air was stifling, and the dust of bones and battles danced in the wind whispering ghostly taunts through the twisting tunnels. I was in that waking-dream state that comes upon you when you've been deprived of sleep and pushed the body to its breaking point. I felt thick of limb and speech, and the heat and wind worked on me like a petrifying agent. It was in this altered state that we waited for Forest.

Noon came and passed, and we waited. The sun moved across the sky, and we waited; the heat became intolerable, and we waited; we became thirsty and ill-tempered, and still we waited. After about three hours, we gave up on Forest and left the Coliseum. Europe was like that. You'd meet people, have incredible times, plan to hook up, and if it happened it happened. Dejected and worn-out, we hailed a taxi and told the driver to take us to a hotel near the Spanish Steps. We weren't in the room for more than a minute before we passed out on the bed. Sixteen hours later, we awoke burned out and bedeviled.

We've spent the last few days bumming around St. Peter's Basilica and the Vatican Palace. After the "Last Escapade," we decided to take things real easy. Everything is relaxed and very mellow. The only thing that really got a rise out of us was all that Papal loot. There seemed to be gold, jewels, and priceless art everywhere. It really is almost beyond anything you can imagine. Yet, even though it's omnipresent, you get the feeling that the real treasure is down one of the roped-off corridors, or hidden away in a secret underground vault.

Like everybody else, we got a little stiff-necked trying to study the ceiling of the Sistine Chapel. It really is hard to imagine how anyone, including the great Michelangelo, could have accomplished such a feat. The artistic vision it embraces, the sheer scope and magnitude of the work, everything about it leaves you in awe. In truth, it only could have been commissioned by a Pope and completed by someone driven by divine powers.

Gina told me she's had a premonition, a vision of sorts. She's convinced that something bad is going to happen. She doesn't know if it's going to happen to her or me or both of us, but she's had dreams about dying. She says we're being followed by a big black crow and people are giving us the evil eye. One thing's for certain, Gina doesn't look good. She's really somber, almost penitent, and begun wearing a silver necklace with a tiny cross she twists nervously around her index finger. There are dark circles under her eyes, and she's lost a lot of weight. She was okay until we got to the Vatican. That's what got to her. I think she did this big self-examination thing and convinced herself she's sinking in sin. I think she even went to Confession. The other day she disappeared for about an hour and I bet that's where she went.

Maybe I've pushed her too hard. Yeah, I've definitely pushed her too hard. I took her in way over her head. I'm a no-good bum and a heel, that's what I am. I'm going to do a total shutdown, a complete and total shutdown. No more drugs and no more booze. All that shit is poisoning our souls. We've got to slow down and clean up our act before it kills us.

We're getting out of Italy today. We'll take the train south, just like we planned; south to Brindisi and then the overnight boat to Greece. No more drugs and booze, just lots of sun, rest, and good food. I owe Gina that; I owe her more than that. Yeah, no more drugs and booze, that'll be our mantra!

Yeah, things will be different in Greece. We'll eat goat cheese and olives. We'll go to the Acropolis and the Parthenon and dig all those pagan statues. We'll make love again, just like we used to. We'll stand in front of all that Olympic nakedness, make love and forget all about Rome.

Things will be different in Greece. They've just got to be.

We're on the train that's taking us to Brindisi, it's very hot, and I'm soaking in sweat. We couldn't get a sleeper and we're in a cramped little compartment. Gina's sitting across from me and I can see her through my eyelashes.

I'm having the strangest waking dream; it's more like looking through a window into a possible future. I find myself standing in a little church, maybe a chapel, and except for a small simple chair in the center of the room, it's empty. Gina's there, too. She's sitting in the chair and in her lap is a baby. I'm standing right in front of her, but she doesn't seem to see me. She's holding the baby close to her breast, and it looks so safe and secure. I'm calling out her name and waving my arms right in front of her face, but nothing happens. All her attention is focused on the baby, like I'm not even there. Then, as I reach out to touch her, the vision disappears, and we're back in our sweaty compartment.

The train pulled into the port of Brindisi a few minutes ago and, at this moment, we're walking across a huge concrete square covered with gull droppings and the bleached remains of fish. Pelicans dip into the green brine, and old sea hands tether the ferry to fat, rust-flaked bulkheads that run along the edge of the dock. The air is singing with bells and excitement. The gulls are screeching overhead, and there's the laughter of anticipation as hundreds of people carrying scuffed-up suitcases, boxes wrapped with twine, and packages of speckled cheese, climb across the sea-blackened plank that takes us onto the cherry and white Apollonia. Maybe it's the smell of the sea, or the thought of sailing into the misty Greek Isles, but Gina has been revitalized. In the sunlight she appears angelic and I can almost believe in the possibility of love and redemption.

We've left the port behind and put out to sea. The bottom level of the ferry is jammed with cars; the upper two levels are crammed with hundreds of passengers either strolling the decks or inside the restaurant. Climbing up to the top deck we can see the harbor lights fading behind us as dusk begins to fall. Up ahead, the sky is slashed by jagged streaks of purple and pink.

After watching the sunset we struck up a conversation with Heloise and George, two beefy-cheeked Canadians.

"We met at work," George said with an affability that made you want to be his best friend.

"At the Canadian Pacific Railroad," Heloise chirped, flapping her arms like a bird in distress. "I had just moved to Vancouver and George was my supervisor."

"She caught my eye straight off."

"Straight off? It took you six months to ask me out!"

"But look at us now," George said, scratching his head and grinning like a teddy bear, "on our honeymoon."

It was terribly romantic to see the way they looked at each other and were always holding hands. They're a lot older than we are, maybe in their early thirties. When they asked if we were planning to marry, we smiled and chuckled awkwardly. This was something we had never really talked about, but I could tell by the look on her face that Gina had begun thinking of us in that way. Why not? George and Heloise seemed happy enough.

At that very moment, the ferry began to rise and fall and the inside of my stomach tightened up into a knot. My head was swimming in nausea and, before I knew how it happened, I was bending over the rail, heaving my guts into the wind. I had never been seasick, but after it was over and I had washed up, I felt surprisingly well. I was clear-headed, although a little weak, and Gina suggested that I try some hot broth. Once inside the restaurant I could hardly feel the boat moving at all. George and Heloise joined us and we sat down on a crowded bench attached to a long wooden table. I listened to them talk politics with a couple of left-wing, Italian university students and some half-crocked Danish Socialists on their state-paid vacation. As I sat there, sipping my broth and nibbling on a biscuit, one of the Danes went off on a long tirade about the Death of God.

"First there was Nietzsche with his Zarathustra coming down from the mountaintop discovering, quite to his astonishment, an old saint still looking for God. Well even if God wasn't dead then, after the Holocaust how can anyone still believe in Him? All that unspeakable horror and suffering, what kind of God let's that happen? What kind of God do you believe in after that? You tell me. If God existed, he died in the Death Camps."

As the words trailed off, I slipped away from the table and walked out onto the deck. Night had fallen, the sea was calm, the air cool and invigorating, and the sky a black canopy peppered with fat stars. I settled down into a stiff lounge chair that was backed up against the cabin wall and pulled a coarse wool blanket over my legs and chest. Shielded from the rising breeze, I eased a small leather-bound journal out of my breast pocket and began to write.

TO THOMAS JEFFERSON

Floating upon the swollen sea,
I saw amber puffed mounds,
Pitch and fall from the depths,
Summoning petulant sea birds,
To navigate my course.

All the way, wearily, wearily,
I penned manuscripts of slop,
And conjured the weary Hercules,
Carrying argosies of gallant men,
To wed the jealous sea.

"Cup the orient sun," he cried.
"Beckon the burgeoning moon,
Hosted by her star brigade,
To kiss the polling booths,
From New York to Athens."

Oh, the cannibal splendor:
Obscene fat men smoking cigars,
Moonstruck lovers sucking dove's eggs,
All singing merrily, merrily,
To Thomas Jefferson.

By the time I finished the poem, Gina was at my arm and I pulled her under the blanket. We spent the night talking dreamily about our future together and about someday having a family. It seemed, once again, we were headed on a course that would bring us safely through the dark night of our relationship.

We were awoken by the sun as it peeked over the rim of the world and lit up the wine-dark sea with orange sparks of fire. Egypt was somewhere to the south, Albania due north, and directly ahead - the Greek Islands. Later that morning, images of warring

Greek gods and Homeric heroes sailing to Troy danced before my eyes. Across the diamond-backed waves I could hear the Sirens calling out for Odysseus and in their call I heard my name being sung, only this time it was on the lips of olive-skinned princesses riding over the swells on silver-finned dolphins.

I pulled Gina close, gazed out across the spellbinding waters, and found myself sinking into a dreamlike trance, as if I were recalling a dormant memory from the past. I was standing in a large empty room in front of an enormous fireplace. Then quite unexpectedly, I saw a face I knew, a face that had once been as familiar to me as my own, gazing back at me from the depth of the climbing flames. For perhaps five minutes I stood before the flames and the transfiguring face as it radiated a pure golden corona as dazzling as the sun. Gradually the light turned amber, then violet, and then an intense white encircled by rays of the purest yellow. The form stayed in view for about ten minutes, and then out of the flames came a voice of such magnificence and indescribable beauty that I wanted to jump right out of my body and merge into the sound and living radiance. At that instant, I felt a million points of light pierce my mind and a joyous exaltation filled my soul. I became engulfed in a wave of flaming ecstasy that was more intense than any passion I had ever known. As the indescribable voice swept over me, I became filled with a breath of fire purifying my body and mind. It was an exhilarating moment of mystery, power, and rapture.

In the heat, sweating and shaking, I found myself on my knees, beseeching this miraculous power to help me find some meaning and purpose in my life. Then the voice fell into a whisper, and the whisper fell into a silence, and the silence was deafening. I could feel the voice burning in my mind and, without words, the voice said that I had to go into the darkest groves and grottos of my soul until I found redemption and forgiveness. And then I heard the voice sing out like a trumpet through the heavens:

"Give succor to the dishonored, the deprived, and
the sick of spirit - to all who have been disfigured
by negativity, divisiveness, and rejection of the
Good.

"Know this to be true: Each generation that comes
into Being has the power to transform the world
and all its inhabitants.

"Let My Voice be your own. Sing out morning,
noon and night, and your Voice, which is Mine,
will echo in the Voice of the world."

Then, just as I felt as if I were entering into a state of
heightened consciousness and awareness, I felt my mind implode
within the form of my fragile being. Suddenly there was only
darkness and confusion. The dazzling vision had vanished, and I
became small, frightened, and ordinary.

A sharp jab to the ribs brought me out of my trance, and I
thought I heard Gina say: "What do I have to do to get some
attention around here?"

Instantly everything sort of flip-flopped; the recollection
became hazy, then evaporated, and once again I was back on the
Apollonia looking out over the city of Patras. As the ferry docked,
we spied George and Heloise waving to us from the deck below.
By the time we caught up with them, much to our surprise, we
discovered that they had rented a car.

"Why don't you come with us?" George bellowed. "I like to
drive, really, I do."

"Certainly he does," Heloise added, grabbing Gina by the
arm. "It would be fun."

"Are you sure?" Gina said, looking my way tentatively.
"Wouldn't it be too much trouble, taking us all the way to
Athens?"

Before I could even think it over, George had me in a bear hug, and Gina and Heloise were walking merrily away from the dock. Minutes later we were in a tiny Morris Minor winding our way through pushcarts and donkeys, following a tree-lined road that spiraled lazily into the surrounding hills thick with wildflowers and olive trees. Soon we were traveling southward on Route 9, along the rocky coast which curved slowly back to the east. George figured the trip to Athens would take about a week or so, including stops for sightseeing.

After an hour or two we stopped for lunch and to stretch our stiff legs; we ate hurriedly and rushed off to Olympia, our first destination. Legend and lore suggest that Zeus, King of the Gods, instituted the Olympic games; it was in his honor that these mortal counterparts were initiated in 776 BC. We walked languidly among the ruins of the stadium, guessing where the wrestling, races, and games took place, and trying to imagine what it would have been like to have participated in this ancient spectacle. Then, while Gina and Heloise did an impromptu 50-yard dash, I challenged George to beat me in the triple jump.

We amused ourselves with these antics until we had worn ourselves out. After spending another ten minutes posing as statues, we climbed back into the Morris Minor and drove southeast to the Temple of Apollo. It took us about an hour to reach the inland plateau. When we arrived, we were stunned by the stark solitude of the area and the magnificent Temple of Apollo rising up from the ruins. Almost 2500 years ago the people of this region had faced annihilation from an epidemic of cholera. They attributed their recovery to the intervention of Apollo, and to honor the god they built this miraculous Temple.

As we got out of the car and began making the ascent to the Temple grounds, we tried to imagine how the suppliants felt as they carried offerings up the steep incline that led to the heavens and to the home of the gods. Atop the plateau, we marveled at how well the Temple in contrast to the Olympic Stadium had been preserved. Most of the wide columns were still standing and, as we surveyed the sweeping hills and valleys that opened up before us, we understood why this site had been chosen. It felt as if you could touch the clouds, and it wasn't difficult to imagine the vast power that once emanated from these consecrated stones.

I was just letting my mind wander, looking intently into the brilliant sky, when I noticed a small silvery cloud pulsating with a glowing intensity. Suddenly and wonderfully, I felt as if I were being drawn into the subtle connectedness of things. Then, for one ephemeral instant, all my thoughts stopped. In that instant of perfect peace, I felt my atoms spreading out like a rainbow across the infinite heavens, racing on the wind, bouncing off the rocks and the sun-blanched marble. I had opened every pore of my being and been transformed. In that one fleeting moment, I became a protean character of imagination and poetry. I was the Devil and Christ and the primeval ooze of life.

I felt as if I were standing at the center of existence where time and space, matter and light converge, where I could communicate with flowers and trees, insects and birds. I felt attuned with all living beings, attuned to a spiritual frequency of empowering lucidity and bliss. At that instant, I believed, truly believed, that if I could sustain this miraculous feeling and bring it back with me into the ordinary world, I could end hunger and poverty, intolerance and war. I could transform the utter ordinariness which passes for my life and make it into something of enduring beauty. I could become a man instead of a dot on a page with five billion other dots. If I could only find a way to take this euphoria back with me into the world from which I had come, I would scream: "This is what it means to be alive!"

But that moment and that way of knowing things could not be maintained. The world around me soon became a chaotic and meaningless blur of lights and sounds. My mind ached with a throbbing density, and I felt as if I were being pulled downward like a meteor hurtling through space and crashing into the earth. I was a lost soul. My sense of Self had been shattered into a thousand shards sprinkled across the unforgiving terrain, and then the world went into a spinning blackness. Gradually, breath by breath, second by second, I returned to my ordinary consciousness and found myself kneeling near a tall fluted column. The stars had grown dim, and the sky dark with the threat of rain. A few more minutes passed before I summoned the strength to join the others at the base of the plateau. At George's urging we decided to leave the Temple of Apollo. As we drove into the darkness, I sunk into a deep depression. I felt as if I had lost the best part of me, the only living part of me, and all that remained was the hollow trunk in which my soul once dwelt.

We stopped for the night at a nearby village, but I just couldn't fall asleep. I just laid there and watched the movie of my life play out before me. I got up this morning tired and exhausted from the struggle. That's how I felt as I climbed into the back of the Minor and we took off for Sparta. I sat in the back snuggling against Gina and tried to sleep, but it was impossible. As I took in the vista of rolling hillsides, I recalled that in the ancient world the city-state of Sparta was renowned for its military discipline. In ambition and power it even rivaled Athens. I had read somewhere that the road *to* Sparta was covered with the swords of fallen heroes and the blood of conquered armies. I always thought that it must have been the other way around; surely it was on the road *from* Sparta. Perhaps it is all in the way one looks at things. Nonetheless, for me this road will always be remembered as a place of broken dreams, a lonely passage through the barren landscape of my life, a place upon which nothing of enduring beauty might grow.

As I gazed out over Mt. Taygetus, I realized that something devilish and dwarflike was growing inside of me, and my capacity to love was overmatched by this older and more powerful force. I wanted to love Gina and to surrender completely to that love, but the more I tried, the more I convinced myself this was possible, the deeper and more completely I felt myself drifting into chaos. I tried to rid my mind of these troubling thoughts, but I knew that one day there would come a terrible moment that would tear us apart, a moment for which I could neither prepare nor forestall.

One thought led to another and soon I was thinking of the ancient Oracle at Delphi who, sitting atop a crack in the earth, would become intoxicated by the holy fumes and answer questions about the future. But the Oracle's pronouncements were so cryptic and perplexing that their meaning had to be interpreted by the person who asked the questions. Maybe I was misreading the signs. Maybe, just maybe, love would conquer and rule over my wavering heart.

We just hit a rock in the road and the jolt drew me out of my daydream and threw Gina into my lap. As I held her in my arms, I made up my mind to carry on with all the joy I could muster. When and where the inevitable would strike was out of my control, and even if I could sense disaster and ruin in the background of everything that was happening to us, I vowed to move into the future as if I were unaware of our fate.

Later that morning we visited the city of Sparta, but George seemed very disappointed with the bustling metropolis. When we stopped for lunch, he told us why. "When I was just a little bugger," he paused for effect, holding up his thumb and index finger about an half inch apart, "my Grandpa would tell me stories about the war between Athens and Sparta. I always dreamt that one day, I'd walk across the training grounds of the great Spartan army."

Our waiter, who had just served us a platter of lamb and rice, had apparently overheard George's lament. "Sirs - please don't think me impolite - but just a few kilometers to the north are ruins, just like the ones you're looking for."

Well after hearing that, George rushed us through lunch and soon we were back in the Morris Minor. Although we spent the better part of the afternoon trying to find the ruins, we were unsuccessful. After much needling and downright pleading, Heloise convinced George that we had done enough trudging round the hillside for one day. Reluctantly, he abandoned his search, and we took some lodging for the night at a small, quiet, roadside hotel.

Our blue-hued room was comfortable with a large inviting bed and a thick, woven, flotaka rug. Gina seemed lost in her own thoughts, and that was just as well. We spent the evening sipping earthy wine, writing letters, and washing our clothes in the bathroom's wide marble sink. Before we slipped beneath the covers we exchanged mutually appreciated foot rubs. A soft, gentle peck on the lips followed this show of concern; then I turned off the lights and for a long time listened to Gina sleeping. What a wonderful sound she made, so at peace, so serene and secure. It was hard to imagine that anything could ever disturb such slumber. I closed my eyes and tried to enter into the rising and falling flow of her breathing, but like all the good I wished for this too was denied. Ruefully and solemnly, I looked out the window and gazed at the deepening shadows. It seemed to me that the world and everything in it was under the magic spell of forgetfulness, everything and everyone except for me.

TIME TRANSPOSED

And this is the judgment,
that the light has come into the world,
and people loved darkness rather than light
because their deeds were evil.

Gospel of John

It feels like a million years ago since we left the States. I've changed. Gina's changed. The universe has changed.

It's four in the morning, Gina's asleep beside me, and my mind is reeling with lurid images of her and De Kooning. As if that weren't enough torture, I've been possessed by haunting visions of the death camp at Dachau, and a few minutes ago I looked at my arm and thought I saw a train of ants boring bluish numbers into my flesh.

Who am I? What have I become?
I'm a loathsome monster swimming in a sea of anxiety, slithering silently across the icy depths, endlessly waiting for one penetrating ray of light to pierce the solitude and lead me upward through the murky shadows. I'm living in a hideous zone of intertwining realities.

When we were in Barcelona, in the Church of Santa Maria, Gina told me she believed with all her heart that Jesus had died for our sins, but I'm not sure that's what really happened. I think we crucified him because we could not believe that each of us could really be like him. He was a mirror that gave us a reflection of what we might become, and by comparison we were horrified and ashamed of what we were. It's one thing to *believe* in God, and quite another to *live* as Him. Then and now, this is our blessing and our curse: We must either become like God, or kill Him.

We've been in Greece for almost a week, and even though it's another warm sunny morning I'm freezing. I tried a hot bath, but it didn't help. I think I'm frozen from the inside out, like something you dig up from the ground. Gina's not in our room. I can't imagine where she is, unless she's at breakfast with George and Heloise. *George and Heloise*. How did I let them talk me into this odyssey in the first place? The first chance I get I'm ditching them - car or no car. I'd do it right now if it weren't for Gina. She's taken a liking to them. In fact, she and Heloise have bonded like sorority sisters. Most of what they talk about irritates me, but it keeps Gina smiling, and I think it's preventing her from seeing what a grouch I've become.

I found Gina in the hotel's tiny cafe and we're having breakfast - the *four* of us. I've already had enough coffee to last me from summer through winter, but I'm still freezing, and now I'm jumpy as a rabbit. Even though I've promised myself to act as cheerfully as possible, I'm not sure I can get through another day with George and Heloise.

I keep thinking about yesterday's expedition for the lost soldiers of Sparta, how George kept pouting and Heloise kept stroking his head calling him "Georgie, poor Georgie," and telling him he was a "better little soldier than any of those old Spartans." It made me sick to watch her fawn over him that way. Everything they do is getting on my nerves - especially the handholding! Worse than that, they've taken up the nauseating habit of feeding little forkfuls of food to each other. If they keep it up, I may have to poison them.

I've managed to drag everyone away from breakfast and out of the inn. We're on the road to Mycenae, and Gina and I are wedged into the Morris Minor's cramped back seat. All I can see are the backs of the lovebirds' heads, so things don't seem quite so bad. I bet they're holding hands in the front seat, and that bothers me, but since I don't have to see it it doesn't seem so awful. Ten minutes ago I would have made George drive straight through to Athens, but now with the sunshine pouring in I'm finally starting to warm up.

Since we arrived in Greece, Gina's been looking better, and that makes me happy. She's regained a little weight and the circles under her eyes have started to fade. There's something else going on, but I'm not sure how to describe it. She's begun giving off a warm, radiating glow of contentment. For the moment, it feels as if the great thaw is coming on, and the ice that has swallowed up my soul is melting away. I'm certain that this small rebirth will not last very long, but while it does I'm going to gorge myself on all the pleasures the day has to offer. Nothing more is going to bother me. The sun is shining, the birds are singing, and I am euphoric and resolute.

George just turned around and told us that we'll be arriving in Mycenae in a few minutes. In that tiny bubble of time I'm scribbling my new credo.

SONG OF THE DAY

I am alive in the song of the day.
I surrender to the melody.
I revel in harmonic overtones.
I thrill to the sound of my own call.

I find measureless joy in music:
A pleasure as honest as laughter;
A recognition as strong as love.

Doubts, I have many.
Yet I know -
Creation is one long note,
Renewed in celestial rhythms.

In my death, may I merge into
The great Eternal Ping:
My bones strung like galactic chimes,
My flesh transformed into the rush of wind.
And my soul? Let it turn to the earth
And rejoice in the hum of insects.

A peculiar and astonishing thing happened today. We had spent the morning touring the ruins of Mycenae, the five-thousand-year-old city made famous by Heinrich Schliemann who excavated the site in 1874 and found what he believed to be the golden mask of King Agamemnon. It was an important find and elevated Schliemann (who was already renowned for his earlier discovery of the lost city of Troy) to the status of a world celebrity.

We were just walking around the tombs, talking about old Schliemann, and wondering aloud about the treasures that were once buried there. We were having a merry old time of it, but just as George and me began chasing the girls around yelling, "Agamemnon is gonna get you," we noticed we were being scrutinized by a slight, balding, older man, dressed in one of those archeological outfits you see in the National Geographic Magazine. Apparently, he had been eavesdropping and shadowing us for some time, because when he saw what we were doing, he suddenly stepped forward and began admonishing us in an old-fashioned, stentorian way. Wagging a finger in my direction, he told us that the tomb of Agamemnon was not a playground, adding sternly, "You would do best to tread lightly on these ancient grounds, lest you bring down the wrath of the gods."

We looked on incredulously as he introduced himself as Professor Ignatius Tulip of the Aristotelian University of Thessaloniki. Then he asked, quite gravely, if we were unaware of the curse that the gods had laid down upon the House of King Agamemnon. For the next hour, we sat attentively and respectfully on an adjacent grassy knoll as Professor Tulip mesmerized us with a fantastic tale of murder and revenge. He described in vivid detail the return of Agamemnon after the Trojan War, how he had been butchered in the bath by his Queen, how their son in turn murdered her, and how the poor, hapless boy had been hunted down and tormented by the avenging Furies.

The point of his tale was to underscore his warning that the ground upon which we walked so cavalierly was quite cursed. In that aim, he succeeded quite admirably; Heloise and Gina were quite shaken, and I think that gave him some real satisfaction, for when he saw the effect of his performance the diminutive scholar walked off in a triumphant trot. I couldn't help chuckling as I watched him saunter up the hill. Yet I was taken aback when he whirled around at the top of the rise, and, before disappearing, pointed menacingly right at me shouting, "Those whom a god wishes to destroy he first makes mad."

The rest of the day, by comparison, was serene and uneventful. We continued on our tour, winding our way around the crumbling city walls and the horseshoe-shaped amphitheater, but now we did so with a newly found reverence. The only other disturbance came as we were heading back to the car. For a joke, I stepped into the theater's stone semicircle and began performing a bawdy parody of Agamemnon in the bath. Well, that really got Gina steaming.

"Jonathan West . . . I don't see the humor in this at all! You think it's funny to be betrayed and murdered by someone you love?"

"But it's only a myth . . . a fantasy . . . that's all it is."

"Fantasy or not," she fumed, "You've no right to mock these kinds of things. It's a terrible thing to find out that all you believe in has been a lie. You'd be much better off remembering what Professor Tulip said."

I bit my lip and nodded my head in agreement, but the comic image of the little professor got the best of me. I did everything I could not to laugh and that only made Gina angrier. She started on about the evil eye and the work of the Devil. Then, as a gesture of finality, she said something under her breath in Italian, made the sign of the Cross, and ran to the car.

By the time I caught up to her, she had locked herself inside. It was through rolled-up windows that I made my best apologies.

"I'm sorry . . . honest . . . I was wrong, and I promise never again to tempt the wrath of the gods. C'mon, Gina, let me in, I'm really, really sorry."

After a few more minutes of contrite yodeling, she rolled down the windows an inch or two, and turning to me with tears in her eyes said, "I'll forgive you, because . . . I love you . . . but sometimes I just don't know what possesses you."

George and Heloise took in the whole episode in their usual good-natured way, and after advising us to "kiss and make-up," we were off again in the little Morris Minor. In the course of the next hour, I endured some railing from Gina and learned from Heloise more than I ever wanted to know about the history of Vancouver, but through it all I was very happy. It was the first day in quite a while that I had a sense of well-being and contentment. I was among friends who cared about me, wanted to protect me, and wanted me to share deeply in their lives. Maybe the Professor was right . . . maybe there would come a day when I would be hounded and hunted and driven mad - but it would not be today, and for that I was most thankful.

About six in the evening we checked into the Astir, a modest, family-owned hotel furnished in traditional Greek. The sweltering heat wave that had been predicted failed to materialize, and that has made everyone carefree and lackadaisical. After we checked into our room and cleaned up, we had a delicious dinner of fresh seafood and yogurt dishes at the Minos taverna. Following that, we attended an open-air performance of Aristophanes' comedy, *The Clouds*, presented as part of the annual summer festival.

When the performance ended, Gina and I agreed to meet George and Heloise at nine the following morning in the lobby of the hotel. With that bit of business concluded, we went our separate ways into the warm and fragrant night, walking through voluptuous meadows and serpentine fields pulsating with cicadas and tremulous fireflies. It was one of those magical nights when you felt as if you could walk forever. Hand in hand we circled through the hillside, floating over stardust bridges and vine-covered ruins until we found ourselves back again at the hotel. We spent the rest of the night sitting on the terrace, contentedly drinking wine and gazing at the stars.

It was perfection, and I wish we could have always stayed that way. I don't think Gina ever looked as happy and secure as she did that night. If ever we had found one moment worth keeping and sustaining, this was it. We sat there for hours, so caught up in each other that we didn't notice the bank of clouds that had moved in from the sea until a drop of rain hit Gina in the eye and sent us scurrying into our room.

Through the night and into the morning, while the rain fell like sweet music we held on to the hope of love, and for the first time in weeks I found the true serenity of sleep. It was almost midday when the rain finally stopped and we got out of bed and went downstairs. The sun was trying to break out from behind the last remaining clouds, and when it did the entire world was born anew: a glistening landscape of vibrant greens, chromium yellows, and purple blushes. George and Heloise soon joined us for brunch, and as the village came back to life around us, full of joy and optimism we loaded up our gear and wheeled onto the road that led to Athens.

"What a mess," George groaned, "the traffic is unbelievable, unbelievable!"

We've arrived in Athens at rush hour and everyone is driving at breakneck speed, switching lanes, cutting each other off, even driving up on the sidewalk. In addition to the cars and buses, there are a zillion people weaving their way through the maze, some on foot, but most on bicycles and mopeds. The heat wave everyone's been waiting for has finally hit. It feels like it's a hundred degrees, and even though it's hot enough to melt glass, most of the women are draped in long, black-cloth dresses.

It's a real nuthouse! No one uses any turn signals. People are waving their arms frantically out their windows, cursing at each other, but you can't hear what they're saying because everything is drowned out by the incessant blare of horns. We're momentarily stuck behind a caravan of dirty buses, and the exhaust fumes are so bad that Heloise and Gina are choking. We've rolled up the Minor's windows, but with no air conditioning we're suffocating. Then George, red as a brick, explodes. "This place is crazy! Crazy! They sure don't drive like this in Vancouver!" Smacking him on the shoulder, I add, "Georgie boy, they don't drive *anywhere* like this."

We just hit a big traffic circle with a marble monument in the center. Hundreds of people, seemingly marooned, suddenly dart out into the traffic. It's pandemonium! Heloise has a map of Athens spread out across the dashboard, and between coughs and sneezes is yelling, "George, get to the right . . . go straight . . . swing to the left." Then Gina screams: "You've got the map upside down! Go to the left . . . now make a right!" Suddenly, we're careening off the circle and down a steep narrow street barely wide enough for a skinny cat. I don't know how he did it, but George got to the Grande Bretagne Hotel without getting us killed. Even though we should be totally wiped-out, our adrenaline is keeping us going. Crazy as it may sound, we decide that after we've checked in and cleaned up, we're going exploring and out for a night on the town.

On the elevator ride up to our rooms, Stavros, our porter, goes into his spiel. "Just arrived in Athens, today? How fortunate! How lucky! Tonight they open the new show at the Acropolis." Then with a pitchman's skill he adds, nonchalantly, "If you should like to go - my cousin Dimitri can get tickets, *special* tickets - the *best* tickets." Then as we arrive at our floor he adds with a winsome smile, "I already like you so much that I will be your personal guide - no extra charge!"

Well call it luck or fate, we decide to take Stavros up on his offer and agree to meet him downstairs in the lobby at eight. Our suite is in the *unrenovated* part of the hotel, but it's spacious and immaculate. The GB, as it's known, was once the "in place" for the international political crowd, and even though the furniture is pretty old-fashioned, the hotel does have has a certain distinguished air. We really only have a short time to unpack, shower, and dress, but we do so with the practiced skill of seasoned travelers.

While Gina is finishing up, I decide to check out the street scene in front of the hotel. The traffic has died down, but the city seems to be alive with an undercurrent of frantic energy that jumps at you from every open window. Everyone's talking very intently and with great passion. They're all speaking Greek so I can't understand anything they're saying, but strangely enough that doesn't seem to matter. I'm happy just to hear the sound of their animated voices. Then I notice the soldiers - they're in full military gear, brandishing rifles, and walking in units of four. Some are stationed on corners with walkie-talkies, but most of them are milling along the sidewalk with the rest of the crowd. It's really odd and a little frightening, but odder yet is the fact that no one seems to notice them. It's as if they're invisible; they don't even get a second glance.

Oddest of all, there are no women on the street. They've disappeared! All I see are men. Even in our hotel - they're all men, wearing almost identical, tight-fitting black pants, and white shirts open at the neck revealing thick chains of burnished gold nestled in black curly hair. It's as if all the women have been locked away and only men and soldiers are permitted to walk the streets.

My musings are suddenly interrupted as I'm joined by Gina, George, Heloise, and Stavros. With a flip of his hand Stavros takes off and we hustle behind him. Once we turn the corner, we pass onto a wide boulevard. I can see the Acropolis rising up before me, and my eyes and mouth involuntarily open wide. I look over to Gina, and she has the same take-a-look-at-that-grin on her face. Suddenly Stavros turns down a crooked side street, and although it seemed like the Acropolis was right on top of us, it takes another ten minutes of fast-paced climbing until we're there.

It's already begun to grow dark and the tall Doric columns of the Parthenon cast long shadows across a rectangular open area in which a thousand or more folded chairs are neatly arranged. As we pass by a harried ticket taker, we scramble down the nearest aisle and take the first vacant seats. Soon the sky is a deep blue-black, and when the enormous overhead light grid is fired up it throws thirty-foot, floating ellipsoids of gold and orange against the rock walls in rapidly changing patterns. Then, from the towering speakers comes a symphonic fanfare of trumpets that gradually evolves into a lush tone poem.

Five figures clad in white robes stride across a six-foot-high stage, each taking on the persona of a god. For the next two hours, as the colors change and shift into increasingly breathtaking patterns, the gods recount in alternating Greek and English, the story of Athens. In a classical-style recitative, the gods describe the city's history and the purpose of the key buildings and temples that wind upward to the Parthenon. The program concludes with a brilliant explosion of color and sound accompanied by a spontaneous wave of cheers and clapping, and again with Stavros in the lead we work our way over to the Plaka district which covers the northeast slope of the Acropolis.

It was almost eleven when Stavros ushered us into a bustling open-air taverna. After we settled in and had ordered some grilled beef, a seafood casserole, and a bottle of retsina wine, I casually asked Stavros what was going on with the military. His reaction was to wave his hand close to his mouth. Then, stealthily, he looked around and drew us in. "Ever since Constantine II came to the throne, Greece has been a mess - the politicians are worse than Zeus! Always arguing, fighting over who's boss. This trouble has been going on for years - scandals, bribery, one prime minister, then another worse than the last. Very bad for me, my family, all the *real* Greeks. Then the army took over . . ."

In mid-sentence Stavros stopped. Some soldiers had halted outside of the taverna. Once they moved out of earshot, he continued agitatedly.

"When *they* took over, it was very bad. Made up their own laws, took away our rights. We fought back . . . they put us in prison. Tortured my father and brother. Beat them with sticks and wire. My father, he was already an old man. He wouldn't tell them a thing, but he couldn't take it, he just couldn't take it."

Stavros looked at us desperately and began sobbing quietly. Gina leaned over and held his hands. We sat in silent stupefaction. What could we say?

A few moments later, Stavros found his voice and told us that his father had died in prison, and that it was only recently, under pressure from the Human Rights Commission of the Council of Europe, that some civil rights had been restored. Antimilitary sentiment was still running high and there had been student and worker riots. In fact, up until the beginning of the summer tourist season the downtown area of Athens had been under a military curfew. The soldiers were there to make certain that no more outbursts occurred, especially near the Acropolis.

All through the evening, even though there wasn't a single soldier in the restaurant, I just couldn't relax. The idea of armed soldiers patrolling the city and looking like they'd blow your head off if you gave them some trouble really irked me. After dinner, I asked Stavros where we could go to get away from the soldiers, but still be near Athens. He told me about the fishing village of Cavouri, some thirty miles to the north. He said it was one of his favorite summertime escapes and, not surprisingly, he added that his cousin Dimitri could get us rooms at a first-rate hotel.

Over an after-dinner coffee, we discussed the possibility of driving to Cavouri. Sadly, George and Heloise told us it wouldn't work. In two days they had to drop off their rental car. After that, they were flying back to London and straight off to Vancouver. Emotions were running pretty high when we realized that tonight was going to be our last night together. Even with all my carping about George and Heloise's lovebird antics, I knew I'd really miss them. In fact, the very idea that they were leaving made me uneasy, for they had been a much-needed stabilizing force. I was growing accustomed to depending on them, and convinced that their protective nature acted as a counterbalance to the dark spot on my soul that was waiting to erupt.

Stavros said he would make arrangements for us to stay at Cavouri if that's what we wanted, adding with a mischievous wink, "And you'll need to rent a car, a really good car, a dependable car . . . not one that's going to break down every other mile. Ah, let me see . . . I know . . . I'll call my cousin Dimitri - the King of Volkswagens!"

Maybe it was the wine or the *good vibes* that come from being around friends, but Stavros really broke us up. I mean, even after all that had happened to him and his family, he could still laugh. And that, at least for the moment, made all my doubts and fears seem petty and insignificant. When we got it back together, Gina asked Stavros to find out what accommodations were available at Cavouri, and I asked him to reserve a VW. We had promised George and Heloise to tour the Acropolis with them in the morning, and I figured we'd firm up our plans for Cavouri later that day when we returned to the G.B.

We finished our meal in great spirits and under starry skies the five of us, arm in arm, wandered tipsily back to the hotel. In a matter of minutes, Gina and me were snuggling under thin summer sheets. I held Gina close and felt innocent in a way I hadn't felt for a long time, and with that wave of innocence came a rush of sleep. As it washed over me I found myself slipping back in time. Suddenly it was 1968 and I found myself sinking back into the misty past, dreaming about California.

California was the Mecca to which we directed our chants. It was the land of myth, celebrated in song, in the news, and in the imagination of my generation as the place where it was all *happening*. I knew, some way, somehow, I had to get there. I had to find out for myself if everything I had heard was true.

My old buddy Lenny felt the same way. You know, it's surprising how a couple of years can change a guy. In Lenny's case, it was miraculous! When he first came home from Penn State, I swear I could hardly recognize him. He didn't even look like the same guy. Man, he had changed an awful lot since our corner-hanging days. First of all, he didn't have a single pimple, and he must have dropped a hundred pounds! What was left was solid muscle. The new Lenny always wore these yellow aviator sunglasses, just like Peter Fonda in *Easy Rider*. But best of all, my friend and good buddy, Lenny Rothberg, received on the eve of his twenty-first birthday, a special gift from his rich, Long Island Grandpop - a brand new, cherry red, Triumph sports car.

It didn't take long to make our plans and preparations. Geez, I mean we were headed to CALIFORNIA! Actually, I don't know how Lenny managed to convince his Mom and Dad to let him go, but it took me a couple of days to convince my parents that I would act responsibly and take care of myself. I didn't need their permission, but I wanted it just the same. Once that was settled, I grabbed an old suitcase, threw in some Jockey shorts, a couple of T-shirts, some jeans, gave my Mom a big kiss, my Dad a firm handshake, and I was history. I was traveling light, busting loose, making tracks, heading out to the West Coast.

By the time we reached Ohio, the country had spread out like a patchwork quilt, just like you see in all those Life magazine photos. The Triumph roared down the road and the heat poured through the floorboard like a baptism of fire. The vibrations alone would have killed anybody over thirty. It was a kick-ass, beautiful way to see America: eighteen inches off the ground, at sixty miles an hour, for three thousand miles. Man, it was a gas! Two best buddies off to California to get some laughs, some action, and a taste of the good life.

Midway through Indiana I took my first hit off this Afghani hash we bought from Cochise right before we left. The smoke burned my lungs and made my eyes water, but I held it down as long as I could, just like Cochise told me to do. As I let it trickle out my nose and watched it flume out the side vent, my brain went kind of sappy and the countryside began sprouting multi-colored marshmallows.

At two a.m. we pulled into this Chicago side street. A bum leaned up against the Triumph and tried to hit me up for some spare change. When I told him to bug off, he pulled out his wang and sprayed the windshield. It was that kind of summer night in Chicago. The Democratic Convention was just getting under way and the streets were filled with cops, radicals, and piss.

That Afghani hash is some powerful stuff and it turned Lenny into a real freak. He was stoned from coast to coast. He was ingenious about it too. He'd light up a little chunk, put it inside one of those Vicks inhalers, and stuff that sucker up his nose. Every half-hour, like clockwork, he'd be inhaling those fumes. Is it any wonder he wore those yellow aviator glasses and laughed a lot?

Neither one of us was laughing when we hit Wyoming. We're flying through these gargantuan mountains and our frigging fan belt breaks. You can believe me when I tell you that my ass was freezing. You ever hear of Little America, Wyoming? There are more frigging trucks there than anywhere in the world, but there ain't no Triumph fan belts. I think we'd still be there if it wasn't for this gnarly old dude in an MGA, who just happened to be passing by at 4:00 a.m., just happened to have an extra fan belt, and just happened to know how to put it on. After he got us going, it occurred to me that God is alive and well, and riding around Wyoming in a maroon MGA.

When we finally got to San Francisco, the first thing we did was look up Cliff McCauley. All through school, when we were growing up, Cliff was the neighborhood genius. He lived right next to Stan's candy store, but his mom didn't let him do much hanging out. We all knew when Cliff grew up, he'd be an astronaut, or a heart surgeon, or something incredible. Cliff was a couple of years older than me. When I was a senior in high school, he surprised us all by moving to the west coast to study film at San Francisco State. He was gonna be another Orson Welles, if you know what I mean. For a brain, he was a pretty right-on guy, and even though we busted in on him without so much as a phone call, he agreed to put us up without any hesitation. Actually, it was one of those incredible, fortuitous coincidences. You see, Cliff was living in this cool apartment, and when we got there he was getting ready to drive down to L.A. That's what I meant by "fortuitous coincidences." He had met this soft-porn actress while shopping for bee pollen in an all-night supermart. It was love at first sight, and now he was hooking up with her for a long weekend, just when we needed a place to crash.

Cliff lived in a third floor walk-up in one of those big, old, pastel Victorian houses you see on all those San Francisco cop shows. The house sat down the street from a big medical center, and you could see the hospital rising up through a stained glass window in the living room. The apartment was really in a perfect location: a short walk downhill led you into Golden Gate Park, and in the other direction, no more than a couple of miles away, was Haight-Ashbury. Cliff hurriedly made his farewells, tossed over an extra set of keys and split. Well, after five straight days on the road we were really beat and in need of serious Z's, and when I stretched out on Cliff's big padded couch it felt like Paradise. I awoke the next day refreshed and ready to go, but when I looked around for Lenny, he was gone. On the fridge was a scribbled note which read, "Jonny, free concert in Speedway Meadows. See you later, A-hole."

I took a quick shower, wriggled into my beat-up jeans, threw on a faded blue T-shirt, slid into my Beatle boots, practically inhaled a bowl of cereal, grabbed the keys off the coffee table, and in a flash was out the door. I had no idea where Speedway Meadows was, and it really didn't matter, 'cause I was on my own for the first time in my life, and I was in San Francisco!

As I flew down the steps and started down the hill towards the park, I felt as if I were in a parade. The air was crisp, the sky vast and blue, and the clouds extraordinarily white. I felt like a little boy who's seeing something wondrous for the first time. It was as if I had passed though a magical door leading into a glorious and beautiful new world. Boy, did I feel GOOD! The sun was smiling its midday smile, and everywhere I looked I saw a thousand young dudes bopping along just like me. The park was alive with children clinging to bright red balloons, and ragged old men clutching newspapers and wine bottles. Everyone seemed to be moving in the same direction, because somewhere out there, somewhere beyond us all, the music was drawing each person into its pulsating center.

I stuck out my thumb, and an old Buick Roadmaster pulled over and opened a massive chrome-detailed door. Without hesitation, I jumped headfirst into the arms of the two most angelic, blonde, blue-eyed, long-legged girls I had ever seen. The ride to Speedway Meadows only took about a minute, but it was a minute in which I relished each bump in the road, each jostle, each nudge and squeeze. It was with real regret that I tripped out of the Buick and said good-bye to my beautiful angels. As I stood there and watched them speed around the next turn, it seemed to me that everyone in San Francisco, in California, in North America, in the whole frigging world was pouring into Golden Gate Park.

Directly in front of me, about seventy-five yards away, I can see the back of this huge, rectangular stage that's maybe forty or fifty feet wide. On both sides are these columns of oversized black boxes rising up like twin towers into the treetops, and flowing out of these speaker stacks is this mind-jarring wave of sound: the cosmic sound of Rock and Roll. Then I see someone dancing atop the column to my left - a cherubic space-cowboy, with hair like Julius Caesar. He's beautiful, and he's wearing a toga and these funky sandals laced up to his knees. He's grooving to the music, stomping and bopping, and waving his arms in imaginary circles around his head. While Caesar's gyrating, I wheel around to the right and push my way through a clump of bushes. When I reach the other side, I see the crowd spread out below - it's incredible! There's a sea of bodies - Hell's Angels and Flower Children from the Hog Farm commune, and stunningly tanned California surfer girls spinning in the sunshine like giant daisies - stretched across Speedway Meadows, weaving in and out of pup tents and teepees like mile-long strands of DNA.

Everywhere I look there's hair - I mean HAIR! Hair in braids decorated with beads and bound up with strips of leather and lace; hair in dangling ringlets and thumbnail curls; hair that tumbles down to the ground in raven rivulets; hair twisted tightly into flaxen buns; hair piled high under sombreros and top hats, and stashed under jaunty sailor caps; shimmering mounds of tangled blonde tresses and blunt auburn bangs; bundles of billowing brunette bushes and expanding black Afros; hair in floppy waxed mustaches, and greasy matted beards, and fat, florid, mutton-chop whiskers.

Then suddenly, I find myself running frantically, running ecstatically up this incline. And when I reach the top of this flat rock I leap out into an ocean of hair, and I'm gone. I'm a zero! A nothing! I've disappeared and been absorbed! I am the hair and the screaming guitars and the rutting sea of flesh. I reach up to shield my eyes from the sun, but the sun's an ivory pipe with the face of Merlin carved into its ancient bowl. The pipe finds my hand, and there's a touch of fire in my throat and a rush of smothering black smoke that takes me up beyond a dead moon. I'm standing on a tottering tree limb at the edge of the universe, engulfed by an eye-searing penumbra. I've entered into a forbidden zone beyond the range of the senses, beyond our reach to recognize and claim as our own.

Then, inexplicably, I'm back in the midst of the quaking crowd, and everyone's flashing the same bewildered eyes. All at once, the stage lights start pulsating wildly, and a girl wrapped in buckskin transfixes everyone. She's cursing and wailing, and blue notes of fire are flying from her mouth straight into my brain. She burns my soul with her song, time stops, and I'm on the brink of madness. Then in a voice more powerful than the smoke or the sun or the screaming guitars, she shouts: "My name is Janis Joplin, and I want you to take another piece of my heart."

Janis is ablaze with lightening and thunder. Giant waves of rain are pouring from her mouth, the sky is transformed into a dark storm of blaring guitars, and ten thousand wounded souls who only a minute ago were a teeming crowd are now running pell-mell in all directions. Janis has disappeared and there's a frantic stampede for cover. Milling through the faceless and foreign mob I feel alone, more alone than I've ever felt before. I'm wet and cold, shivering and scared. I'm lost in a maze of bodies, in a city that until a few days ago was just a dot on a map hanging from a dashboard. Then I remember, I'm staying at Cliff's apartment, and if I can just get back there I'll be safe and everything will be all right.

I'm trying as hard as I can to clear my mind, but it's impossible. I feel like I'm in a sensory fog. I just can't remember how I entered the park. *Maybe, if I can get back to that road* . . . as the thought hits my brain, I find myself walking robot-like away from the stage. I zigzag right and then left, picking my way through the crowd and the newly formed mud holes. The downpour was torrential but short lived. Driven by a howling wind the storm moved quickly out to sea, leaving in its wake an eerie inky darkness and a meadow of mud.

I feel a wave of anxiety sweeping over me as I try to escape from the confusion pushing against me from every direction. I zigzag right and left - walking hypnotically - my eyes never leaving the ground. Then, just for an instant, I look up and they're they are: the two beautiful angels who drove me to the park in their chrome-plated chariot. They're running to meet me, laughing deliciously as they wrap me in their arms and cover me with sweet angelic kisses. Now I'm laughing with them, and as I return their kisses we float effortlessly out onto the glistening roadway. We stand there for what seems like forever, huddled tightly in the billowing wind that whips their streaming blonde hair around my face and shoulders. Just to be this close to them, to smell their hair, their perfume, the essence of their being, makes me giddy. I'm on the verge of hysteria, intoxicated with joy and good fortune.

Just as I begin to regain my composure and find the calm center of my breathing, a monster of a motorcycle roars up and stops directly in front of me. On the bike's arching back is this freak covered with feathers, and behind him, a girl with red hair that's fluttering like fire around her face of porcelain. The girl touches my cheek and with the voice of an enchantress whispers,

"Now is the time to fly. Up and away, up and away with the Featherman and his mate."

Inexplicably, everything is beyond my range of comprehension. I'm the most insignificant creature on the face of the earth. I'm without will and powerless to protect myself. I have no ego and no identity. I'm amorphous, protean, incorporeal. There is no center or anchor to my being, and I feel as if I'm about to float off into the chaotic flux of the universe. My two angels are clinging to me. They're very alarmed and shouting at me, but I can no longer understand what they're saying. It's as if I've been transported to a different dimension and they've become shadowy images. Then in one flashing instant, every fear that I've ever known, draws together like a ball of string stuck in my throat. I'm choking and gasping for air, shaking in paroxysms of fear. I want to run off the rim of the world and drop into space, but instead I find myself surrendering to the beguiling voice of the flaming-haired enchantress and climbing on the back of the Featherman's silver dragon. Then, without warning, the beast lets out a deafening roar and we lurch forward into the night. My hands are buried in a mass of incandescent hair as the bike slings around a hairpin turn, belching fire and roaring at the scattering crowds. We're rocketing toward the moon and the feathered monster is soaring over parked cars and skyscrapers.

As we climb dizzily towards the stars, the very forces of the universe are conspiring against me. I feel my hands growing weak, my fingers tearing at the flaming hair and intangible flying feathers, and then somehow I'm falling. I'm free falling through Space and Time, bouncing clumsily off stars and parked cars and the rain-slick asphalt street. My body and soul are shattered; my existence reduced to a searing pain in the darkness of my mind. Gradually I find myself coming into consciousness and, to my surprise, I see a thousand grinning freaks: Julius Caesar and Janis Joplin, Flower Children and Hell's Angels, surfers, hippies, old men and children, and the Featherman and his mate. As they help me to my feet, they begin to laugh. Everyone's pointing at me and laughing, as if the funniest thing in the history of the world must have just happened. So I start to laugh, but my laughter turns into blinding tears of rage and frustration. Then, just as I'm ready to lash out, the motorcycle explodes in a choking cloud of smoke, and as I begin slipping into a solitary darkness the whole jangling crowd disappears.

In that moment, right before I fell into complete oblivion, I saw white sparks of light dancing before me in inexhaustible patterns, and then the lights began taking the shape of people, and I realized I was no longer alone. My two guardian angels were hovering over me, and we were surrounded by people of all ages and races. Yet, as different as they were, they shared one common trait - they were blind. They were all blind and clinging to me, for I alone had sight. But even though I led the way, I knew not where I was going. I was as lost as they, and in my own way just as blind.

We walked in agony, stumbling over sharp jagged rocks, lost in a thick, rancid cloud of burning air. We moved like a wave of flesh over the dark face of the void, sharing one unifying thought - to find our way back into the Light. But although I longed for illumination and truth, there was something ominous and evil growing inside me that I had to confront and overcome. Until I reached that moment of recognition and clarity, I knew I would continue to wander in the darkness.

Then, suddenly, the throngs of people began changing once more into dancing white sparks of light flying off in a million directions. It was at that moment that I opened my eyes and found myself back in Golden Gate Park, lying face down on the roadway, shivering in a San Francisco wind that cuffed me with a fist of hard rain. My knee was burning and throbbing, and bits of skin, bone, and blood were smeared over the street. Then, quite unexpectedly, I thought I heard someone calling out my name, and when I looked up I saw a smiling face, a pair of bright yellow aviator sunglasses, and two long muscular arms reaching down to hoist me up. I was filled with inexpressible amazement when

I realized it was my friend Lenny. I had forgotten that he even existed. It seemed as if I had lived a lifetime in one day and Lenny belonged to a past that had disappeared forever.

Just as I was on the verge of passing out again, I found myself resting securely in Lenny's arms. The last thing I remember was him hooting in my ear, "Jonny my boy, you look really wasted. What happened to you anyway? Too much *fun* for one day?"

When I reopened my eyes I found myself in a momentary state of confusion and panic. Much to my amazement, I was no longer in the dim past of California with Lenny, but back in the present, back in bed with Gina at the Grand Bretagne in Athens.

The first thing I did was look at the alarm clock; it was six a.m., and it felt like a hundred degrees in our room. To top it off, my head was still throbbing with the sound of screaming guitars and roaring motorcycles. Then I turned to Gina who, unbelievably, was wide awake and staring lovingly right back at me. For a second or two, I actually thought about sex, but it was too damn hot for that, too hot to eat, too hot for coffee, too hot even to think.

A few minutes later, we rolled out of bed and got dressed. By the time we met George and Heloise in the lobby, the heat had everyone in a lousy mood. It was so frigging hot that we decided not to walk over to the Acropolis and instead took a taxi. By the time we got there we were dripping wet, even in shorts and thin white shirts. The stifling heat even got to the taxi driver. As he pulled away he yelled something nasty about Americans and the size of his tip.

It isn't even eight but tourists are everywhere. There's barely a breeze, the Acropolis is covered with a dusty paste of pollution and dirt, and the summer haze is making Heloise wheeze. The Parthenon is just ahead of us on the highest part of the promontory, and Gina spends the entire morning in a steamy, semi-ecstatic flush, describing in minute detail the characteristics of marble statuary, the high relief metopes of the Lapith and Centaur, and the low relief frieze of the Horsemen.

Through it all, even with sweat stinging my eyes and a cloud of gnats invading my nose, I can't help but be moved by the glorious magnificence of the Parthenon. Yet this sense of awe is undermined, not so much by my physical discomfort, but by an increasingly mounting uneasiness. For just like the once-great city crumbling down around me, I feel as if I am in decay, and the more I wander through the ancient ruins, the more heightened my sense of loss and dread becomes. As the wind picks up and whips the heat and dust around the towering stone columns, I hear a deep grunting voice calling to me from the shadowy depths of my being, and malevolent notions begin to bury themselves in the compost of my brain.

Finally - three exhausting hours later - as we leave the Acropolis a momentary sense of relief sweeps over me, but by the time we return to our hotel I'm awash with conflicting emotions. To my amazement, I find myself holding back tears as we exchange a farewell with George and Heloise. I can't help but wonder if we'll ever see them again, and don't suppose it's likely.

When it came to our final goodbye, Gina and Heloise put on quite a show. George had to pull them apart - more than once. It was like a farewell scene from *War and Peace* with the anxious gasping and comic pathos. Then, as Gina hung by my side, we watched somberly as the Canadians inched their away around the corner. Moments later, as if they had never existed, they were gone.

We've just entered the Grande Bretagne and Gina's very upset. She's gone up to the room to wash her face and gather our few belongings while I pick up the Volkswagen. Right now, I'm parked in front of the hotel and can't wait to get away from here. I have this uneasy feeling, a kind of foreboding, that if we ever return to Athens something terrible is going to happen, something that will leave us in disarray and ruin.

Gina just came out of the G.B., and now that we're speeding away from the hotel the air seems cooler and my burdens lighter. It took about thirty minutes before we got out of the city and hit the open road. Finally, with the sea in view, my mood became less melodramatic. Even though Gina had been crying all morning, I thought that things still might work out. We'd be alright, I just needed to get a grip on myself and stop worrying about the future. Actually, things weren't really that bad. We hadn't been boozing it up, and although I still had a fat chunk of the Amsterdam hash hidden away, I hadn't touched the stuff since we landed in Greece. I still had the craving, but with each passing day it grew less intense, and that made me feel like I was regaining some self-control.

Yeah, it sure felt good to be out on the open road, away from the heat and those damn soldiers. All the same, now that it was just the two of us I knew we had to be very careful. Although George and Heloise had become tiresome, to their credit and our benefit, they were watchful chaperones and kept us on our best behavior. With that restraint gone, there was really no telling what might become of us.

I had never driven a VW, and it was a trippy sensation. The Bug was surprisingly peppy, and as it zipped up the rocky coast I started thinking about Chickie Roth, one of my old, doo-wop singing, street-corner buddies. Chickie had bought one of these VW's just before we graduated from high school with the money he made sharking at Mosconi's Pool Hall. Chickie had always been a little flaky, so I wasn't really surprised when he bought a giant, mock, wind-up gizmo, and had it attached to the roof of the *Toy*. (That's what he called the VW.) Chickie loved that car. In fact, up until the time he found out he was 1-A and enlisted in the Marines, he drove it everywhere. But right before he went over to Vietnam, he got rid of it. He never told me why, but I suspected that it had something to do with his new tough-guy image.

Chickie was one of the lucky ones who made it back, but when I caught up to him, he wasn't the same fun-loving goof. Now, he was sporting a couple of nasty tattoos, riding a Harley,

94

and hanging out with the Hell's Angels. One night I saw him go crazy in a bar when a guy we both knew from high school walked up behind him and tapped his shoulder. Faster than you can blink, Chickie whirled around and dropped him with a karate chop to the neck.

Like I said, the guy was an old high school buddy, just coming over to say hello. When Chickie realized what he had done he was really sorry. Luckily, the guy wasn't hurt too badly, although at first he just lay there like a dead man. But after a few tense minutes, he recovered his senses, and as soon as he was able to get up on his feet he was out the door. Afterwards, when things calmed down, Chickie and me sat down to work things out over a couple of beers.

Chickie had a rough time over in Vietnam. He told me a few things that made me want to round up the politicians and generals who sent those kids over there, line them up against a wall, and call out the firing squad. One story, above all the rest, still sticks out in my mind. Chickie told me they had trained him to be an expert in what was called the "silent kill." They would put him and a couple of these specially trained killers out on the edge of maneuvers, just outside their camp. When the boys in the platoon were asleep, his job was to kill, as silently as possible, whatever approached. The "silent kill" was supposed to protect their location. So that's what Chickie did, and he did it well. He took out his share of the Enemy - as well as pigs, goats, monkeys, grandmothers, and babies.

Now, I don't know if this was true or if he was just spinning out some yarn to scare a civilian. But I thought, then and now, that he was giving it to me straight. One thing was certain, the war had really done a number on him. The last I heard, he had moved to San Francisco and was one of the thugs who beat up all those kids at the Stones concert at Altamonte. I really don't know if that was true either, but when I think about Chickie, I like to remember how he was in high school before he joined the Marines, just one of the guys hanging out on the corner, shooting Nine Ball at Mosconi's, and zipping round in his little *Toy*.

The road suddenly veered to the left, and as I downshifted into third gear, my thoughts turned back to Gina. The Bug's windows were wide open and the wind was whipping her hair wildly around her face. She had stopped crying and was smiling back at me, and that filled me with hope and optimism. As we motored up the rocky coastline, we saw the sun-drenched fishing village of Cavouri laid out below us like an impressionist painting by Cezanne with cones, rectangles, and triangles sparkling in incandescent flashes of violet, blue, and green.

We've just finished lunch at a roadside cafe and now we're on the spur that leads into the center of town. Cavouri sits at the edge of the Aegean Sea and is everything Stavros said it would be. There are dozens of small fishing boats, a few commercial rigs, a marketplace, a couple of outdoor restaurants, and one tall, bright red phone booth. The air is cool and fresh, and the smell of the sea is strong and invigorating. Up ahead, I can see the facade of the Atlantis Hotel, sitting on a rocky bluff above Cavouri looking out over the beach and the sea.

As we drive the VW up to the hotel's entrance, two preppy young guys dressed in sailing outfits of starched white and blue run to greet us. One takes the few little bags we've accumulated out of the trunk; the other shoulders my backpack and guides us up the impressive stucco portico. The hotel is done in a nautical theme. The wooden floors are a rich, deep, golden brown, and the bright white walls are covered with compasses and charts, pictures of ships and maps, and etchings of the Cycladic Islands. After we check in, we're led up to our room which looks like a cabin on an ocean liner. It even has two glass portals complete with bright brass trim. As I tip the porter, he advises that dinner will be served at nine, and as he backs out the door with a bow he adds that it will be a *special*, a *very special* dinner, because the new owner of the hotel, Captain Gizikis, will be on hand to greet his guests.

It only took us a few hours to get from Athens to Cavouri. It was just after eleven and Gina and I were really itching to get some sun. It had been a couple of weeks since we tanned up in Sitges, and although we did get some color in Nice, it had faded by the time we got to Rome and went out on our "Last Escapade."

The Atlantis had a beautiful, multilevel, wooden deck with broad steps that led downward to a wide flat beach. After we jockeyed the thick, padded lounge chairs into optimum tanning angles, we helped each other apply glistening gobs of Ban de Soleil and settled in for a few of hours of sunning and snoozing.

It was almost three when I awoke, and as I surveyed the broad beach I saw it had sprouted blue striped umbrellas, tent-like cabanas, and an open-air fruit stand. I turned to Gina and found her sitting upright and staring intently, transfixed by something or someone swimming effortlessly over the waves. Then I saw a figure rising up like Venus from the sea. As the apparition walked out of the surf, I shielded my eyes from the sun's glare and saw a young boy of about sixteen. He was tall and slim with glistening olive skin and a swatch of red silk between his legs. He glided out of the surf and over to the fruit stand, the sea dripping down from his head of black curls as he stood luxuriating in the sun. For a few seconds before he looked away, he seemed to be smiling right at us.

I can't explain it, but I had a strange feeling that I was entering into a critical phase of my life that was beginning with the beguiling smile of this enchanting boy. I felt with every fiber of my being that everything that had happened during the past few months was preparing me for this encounter. Then I felt a twinge, like you sometimes have when a cool breeze comes unexpectedly over you. As I turned my eyes from the sea, I had a horrifying vision of Gina lying in a dark shadowy room, broken and bleeding, calling weakly for help. I shuddered violently, and, as I did, I thought I heard a mocking and cruel laugh reverberating in the depth of my being, as if there were a grotesque presence living inside me, watching and waiting for the right moment to take over. It came and was gone in an instant, and although I knew it was crazy to have such visions and thoughts, I also knew it would be impossible to shut them out, just as it would be impossible not to listen to the evil force inside my soul.

At that instant, Gina turned to meet my gaze, and I could tell by the way she looked at me that she had experienced the same premonition. But all of this happened in the snap of a moment at the boundary of consciousness. Though we were aware that something ominous had happened, it was almost instantaneously out of memory and became nothing more than a vague feeling of uneasiness too trifling to dwell on. We just stared at each other, and then, without exchanging a word, adjusted the angle of our lounge chairs, smoothed out the thick white towels, and settled back into plush comfort.

A few minutes later, just as I was about to drift into a warm dream, I saw the exquisite boy from the beach ascend the wooden stairs like a young god. In his arms was a silver tray of luscious sliced fruit. He stopped for a moment directly across from Gina, and as an older woman covered with thick make-up, and adorned with gold chains and diamond bracelets took some melon off the tray, she patted him affectionately on his glistening thigh and whispered something in his ear that made him laugh, a sweet coquettish laugh that sat lightly on the wind and sailed off into the sun. As he turned away, she cooed, "Nikki, Nikki," and deftly slipped a bluish bank note down the front of his bikini.

That's how we first met, and learned his name, and fell under his spell. Nikki, with teeth like perfect white pearls, eyes as green and brilliant as the sea, and skin as fragrant as hyacinth. Nikki, who comes up to the deck wearing only his sandals and his bikini of crimson silk, bringing fresh fruit to assuage our thirst and tempt our hunger. As he stands near, his beauty is overpowering, and we can't help but love him in an unspoken and secret way that neither of us wants to acknowledge.

Suddenly, a crackling voice exploded over a loudspeaker: "Guests of the Atlantis, the deck is now closing. It will reopen tonight for a special dinner hosted by Captain Gizikis. Cocktails will be served at eight. Please, if you will, the deck is now closing."

As we gather up our towels and slip on matching white terry cloth robes, I can't help but wonder why this Captain Gizikis is so damn important. But as we cut across the terrace on the way to our room, I see Nikki waving to us from the beach and nothing else seems to matter.

After returning to our room, the first thing we did was jump in the shower. It was big enough for both of us, and it had good water pressure - which was rare. It also had one of those showerheads that lets you regulate the flow and pattern of the water. I adjusted it to send out a strong vibrating pulse, and, as the hot spray pounded us, I stood behind Gina working her thick hair into a swirling white foam that flowed over her shoulders and down her back and legs. After she rinsed, we reversed positions. As she worked on my neck muscles, I could feel her softness against my back as her hands went down my thighs and between my legs. She moved slowly, rhythmically, and soon we were pressed together in the steam and heat, bouncing off the wall, careening out of the stall, rolling cross the floor, and slithering onto the bed. We had not made love with this kind of hunger for weeks, and I had almost forgotten how intense the physical bond had been between us. Yet, even in the final exquisite moment when our hunger was fulfilled, my sense of isolation and spiritual emptiness seemed only heightened.

Later, as we dressed for dinner, I watched Gina's reflection in the mirror as if I were seeing her for the first time. I realized that she was the most stunning and sensual woman I had ever seen - a Bottecelli portrait come to life. She was wearing a flowing white tunic and delicate white sandals that accented the tanned fullness of her body. She had pulled her hair up and fastened it behind her head with a pink barrette molded in the shape of a small seashell. As I admired her image in the mirror, she draped a thin strand of pearls around her neck and became a goddess.

It was almost eight o'clock when we left our room and strolled across the deck. To our surprise, it had been transformed into an elegant dining area of white linen tablecloths and flickering candles. The night air was intoxicating, full of warm breezes and jasmine perfume. Everyone was dressed in evening clothes, but it was clear from the moment we walked into view that all eyes were fixed upon Gina. She shone brighter than all the early evening stars and I wasn't surprised when our host, Captain Gizikis, greeted us, took Gina's hand, and put it to his lips.

The Captain was tall and clean-shaven with an aquiline nose and a square chin. He was wearing an immaculate, dress white uniform, complete with gold epaulets, colored ribbons, and shimmering medals that hung dramatically across both breast pockets. He reminded me of someone. Then it hit me! He looked just like De Kooning, the painter from Amsterdam, but without the beard.

All of a sudden my legs went rubbery. Then, as I heard Gizikis and Gina laughing, an intense flash of jealousy swept over me like a wave of heat. As Captain Gizikis invited us to dine at his table, I fought to control my boiling emotions. Gizikis had the waiter sit Gina right next to him, and sat me to her left. As the meal began, I tried to regain my composure and at the same time divine the meaning of every glance that passed between them. All through dinner, I nervously guzzled champagne and made small talk with the other guests. Through this chit-chat, I learned that Gizikis had been a hero in the victorious campaign against the Turks and had called on the people of Greece to form a civilian government. Should Greece ever again return to a full participatory democracy, he was considered a likely candidate for the presidency.

After the main course of grilled lamb and vegetables, the Captain launched into an impassioned address about the current political climate in Greece and his dreams for the future. As he concluded his speech, Gizikis was greeted by a thunderous wave of applause and cheers. When this subsided, he extended an invitation to his guests to enjoy all the beauty and pleasure that Greece had to offer. As Gina and the other guests clamored to shake his hand, I felt a sharp pain over my left eye like a nail being hammered into my skull. I weaved my way through the crowd, found Gina, and told her I had a terrible headache and was going back to our room. I had hoped she'd come with me, but instead, looking starry-eyed, she told me that she'd look in on me after dessert.

When I got back to our room my temples were throbbing. I could feel myself slipping into the same malevolent rage that had overtaken me in Amsterdam, and I fought it with all my strength. Somehow, I managed to find four or five tabs of the Valium I had scored in Florence. I gulped them down and collapsed onto the bed. Throttled by pain and morbid fantasies, I buried my head in the pillows and tried to push the twin faces of Gizikis and De Kooning out of my mind.

After a few tense minutes the pills kicked in and I drifted into an exhausting nothingness. When I awoke a few hours later, I was covered in sweat and consumed by a profound feeling of dread. My brain felt as if it were being eaten away; I was consumed by a maniacal viciousness, and my dwarf-soul wanted to vent itself upon the world.

I stumbled out of bed and tottered through the door possessed with one thought: *Find Gina*. In a few moments I was back on the deck. The party was in full swing, but although I looked everywhere I couldn't find Gina, or Gizikis. As I swooned over the deck rail, I saw them climbing up the wooden steps that led from the beach. As they walked arm in arm across the deck, they waved in my direction. Admirers soon engulfed the Captain, and Gina was able to break away. She greeted me with a peck on the cheek and whispered, "I'm so glad you're feeling better. I'm having the most wonderful time."

For the next hour, I somehow smiled and nodded my way through the meaningless conversation, all the while struggling against the malignant thoughts and impulses that wouldn't leave me alone. Eventually, the candles were extinguished and everyone said their good-byes. In the fragrant moonlight we wandered back to our room, Gina as breathtaking as a fairy-tale princess, and I as ugly and insane as the creature I was fighting not to become.

DANCE OF THE SERPENTS

Just as the slough of a snake lies,
dead and cast away, on an ant-hill,
even so lies this body. Then the self
becomes disembodied and immortal Spirit,
the Supreme Self, Brahma, the Light.

Brihadaranyaka Upanishad

My life has become a grotesque comedy. During the day, I sit and watch as Nikki floats back and forth from the beach with his silver tray of fresh fruit and his glistening body. He's beautiful and irresistible, and just like everyone else I crave him. He has a harem of doting rich widows who fawn shamelessly over him. They're always giving him little gifts and whispering in his ear. Then there's Gina - she gets his special attention. As Nikki moves near, she sits up in her chair and he kneels close enough to kiss her. It takes ten minutes of longing looks, pouting, stretching and wriggling, just to pick a piece of fruit off his little tray. Imagine, if you can, that this routine repeats itself almost every hour. To top it off, every night at dinner I sit in a silent fury as Gizikis performs his mesmerizing act on Gina, followed by an "after-dinner stroll" along the deserted beach. What makes the situation even more absurd is Gina's transformation. Like a flower in bloom, each day she becomes more stunning and sensual, and each night our lovemaking is better than the night before. But all the time, day and night, I'm consumed by jealousy, and in the dark swamp of our bed it feels as if we're no longer alone.

We've been sitting on the deck all morning and Gina is as ripe as a golden olive. There's been no sign of Nikki and for that I'm relieved. But now, at Gina's urging, we've decided to go down to the beach and see if he's at the fruit stand. The sand is hot; it reaches up through my sandals and scorches my feet. After walking a hundred yards my shirt is stained with sweat. We're almost at the stand and as we come around toward the front we see Nikki bending over a crate of dark green melons. He smiles as he places the swollen fruit in an open wooden rack. I guess he can tell that we're hot and thirsty, for as we approach he takes a small, bulbous, dark green gourd off the rack and with a slender tapered knife divides it into three equal parts. Taking the offering from his hand, Gina places the moist pink flesh between her lips and thin crimson lines run down her chin and over her throat. Soon, each of us has eaten of the consecrated fruit, and in doing so have been anointed in an unholy trinity.

Guiding us by the hand Nikki leads us into the surf. Within seconds we're deep in the rising waves, swimming out towards a pair of big black rocks. Nikki dives under the sea and we follow him through a long narrow passage that leads to a deserted cove. As we crawl out of the water onto the warm dry beach we watch in anticipation as Nikki slips off his bikini. Soon, the three of us are intertwined on the smooth sand. My eyes are closed tightly and I don't know and don't care whose lips and hands are running over me like waves of erotic music. Then wonderfully, achingly, all the touching and sliding, all the hissing wetness that stings the tongue with sweet drops of sweat comes to an end, leaving us twisted and tangled like serpents in the sun.

Later that afternoon we swam back to Cavouri beach, and I was surprised at how relaxed and at ease we were; there wasn't even a hint of self-consciousness. We acted as if nothing unusual had happened, as if we were three old friends hanging out together for a couple of laughs. Nikki began unpacking another crate of melons, and we stood talking aimlessly, watching Gina draw tiny circles in the sand with a splinter of driftwood. As I gazed at her meticulous efforts, I had the odd thought that our lives were like those circles, and that no matter how carefully we might design and draw our precious plans they could be washed away by the next big wave. All we could do was to start over again or quit the game all together.

Nikki soon finished and Gina suggested that the three of us drive into Athens and have dinner in the Plaka district. It seemed like a great idea and Nikki was genuinely excited. With our little excursion unanimously approved, we agreed to meet on the portico of the Atlantis in an hour. Gina and I returned to our room, and as we quickly showered and dressed I was overtaken by a mounting sense of anxiety. I think we both knew we had come to a turning point in our lives, but it was too late to change the direction in which we were heading.

Ten minutes later we we're in the hotel lobby waiting for Nikki. It was odd to see him walking up the front steps of the hotel to greet us. We had never seen him in anything but his silken bikini. Seeing him outfitted in the same tight black pants and white open shirt that all the Greek men wore seemed to take away a little bit of his magic. He was still the same Nikki, with the same enticing smile and sparkling eyes, but he looked more grown up than the enchanting boy we had held in our arms just a few short hours ago. I think when he took my hand I knew that things were not going to unfold with the same effortless grace they had done earlier. But the impact of this premonition was soon lost in the sound of our laughter and the rhythmic, putt-putt-putt of the VW.

Gina sat in the front and Nikki in the back leaning forward between us. They both smelled wonderful, and as we turned on the radio and hummed along to the strains of bouzouki music, it seemed that in no time at all we were in Athens, weaving through the traffic, parking the Bug, and walking hurriedly towards the bazaar.

The streets are thick with end-of-the-season tourists, and it seems as if they're all headed up the steps and through the colonnade that leads into the open-air market. As soon as we enter, the number of shops and stalls overwhelms us. Everywhere we look there is a surfeit of brightly woven vests, gleaming brass cooking pots detailed with fishes and dolphins, and intricately carved marble figurines of ancient Greek gods. As we wander from stall to stall, holding up diaphanous blouses and marveling at the golden brocade that's woven into the silk and linen, we're mysteriously drawn into a partially concealed corner of the market. There, draped across the walls, are the most gorgeous sheepskin coats one can imagine. Even though it's hot and terribly humid, Gina and Nikki are soon modeling for me and for each other. As they prance in front of a full-length mirror, their bronze skin offset by the sheepskin's white tufts, I can't decide who's more beautiful. We don't even bother to bargain with the shopkeeper; we want the coats at any price. Somehow he fits both of them into a slim cardboard box, and with the box wedged under my arm we're off to the Plaka.

It's just turning dark when we arrive at the terraced entry of the Hesperides taverna. Our waiter introduces himself as Alexander, seats us at a table near the stage, and then disappears. He returns a few minutes later with an enormous chilled platter of tomato, cucumber, olives, and feta cheese. Alexander can sense that there's something special happening between the three of us and asks Gina if it's her birthday. Before she can even reply that it isn't, he sings out, "Ouzo, ouzo. You must drink ouzo to celebrate. It is the Greek way."

Instantaneously, three small glasses are placed before us. After Alexander fills each with a colorless viscous liquid, he pours himself a shot and places the bottle on the center of the table. As he yells, "Eis Igian," we raise our glasses and, following his example, down the ouzo in one gulp and throw the empty glasses into a massive stone fireplace. As the glasses smash against the stone wall, the anise fire of the ouzo almost knocks me over. The inside of my belly and mouth are burning, my eyes are tearing, and just like Gina and Nikki I'm reaching for the nearest glass of water. Alexander is in an uproar. As he pours another round he shouts, "Again, again! Drink, drink! Nothing like ouzo!"

As the water cools down the fire I can taste the ouzo working into the back of my throat and I feel a little click in my brain that I've never felt before. So it goes, the drinking of ouzo and the dining on moussaka and cheese pies. More ouzo, and roast lamb, and grape leaves stuffed with meat, rice, and onions. Then a second bottle, and sweet custard, and grapes and melons, followed by a third bottle of fire. The lights in the taverna suddenly grow dim as the band and dancers mount the stage. When they begin to play, the world slips a little sideways and I feel as if all my senses have been stretched beyond their capacity and limitation.

Soon, the scene is one of mad delirium. The dancers are shuffling and leaping like wild-eyed beasts, yelling and kicking to the rhythmic strumming of the bouzouki. Faster and faster they spin, like satellites whirling round the earth. Then, without warning, the mad spinning and music halts. In that unsettling moment of silence, Gina and I watch in amazement as the most beautiful and graceful of the dancers slides over to Nikki. He bows before him taking Nikki's face in his hands and kisses him hard on the mouth. Then, in one incredibly smooth and fluid motion, he picks up a table with his teeth, and with his arms spread out like a giant bird he begins to spin around the room. It is then I realize that this is not a man but a god, a god descended from the Olympic heights, and he's come for our Nikki.

The spinning table is a blur and we're up on our feet, dancing shoulder-to-shoulder, sending glasses and plates flying through the air. As Gina falls against me, I see the dancer-god wrap his arm around Nikki's waist and lead him through a glass bead curtain off to one side of the stage. I've taken a half-empty bottle of ouzo off the table and standing dead center in the room amidst the broken glass and overturned tables have raised it to my lips. As the crowd claps and urges me on I drain the bottle dry. I know the blood lust is in my eyes; I am menacing and my dwarf face is there for all the world to see. I'm holding Gina against me so she can't see my face. She can't see the monster I've become as I lead her through the glass bead curtain and up a narrow set of stairs.

At the top of the landing I hear music coming from a doorway at the far end of the hall. We're there in an instant and I kick in the door with one blow. In the dim red light I see Nikki and his lecherous god locked in an embrace of cosmic fire. Then, unexpectedly, in the midst of their struggling they turn towards us and let out a long, inhuman, beckoning groan.

In that unnatural moment, I find myself sinking to my knees, drowning in an ocean of devouring kisses that burn and brand you. Gina's beneath me, pulling me into the deepest part of her, but it's not me who's inside her - it's De Kooning and Gizikis and

Nicki - it's every man who's ever looked at her face and seen the maddening hunger in her eyes. I want to stop. Gina wants to stop. But we can't. We've reached the moment when the deepening ache ignites the match, and nothing in this world can stop us now.

Between the pounding moans and cries Gina tells me that she's never loved anyone but me, and that she's pregnant with our baby. But it's too late for that; too late for love and babies. We've sunk into the muck, pierced each other's flesh and opened all the old wounds. The only thing left for us is to feed upon each other until all the stars implode, until the light that nourishes soul and spirit is no more, until all living things return to the quiescent singularity and dissolve into Nothingness.

I awoke this morning slumped against a rusted-out garbage can in an alley behind the Hesperides, my mind crushed in a cubist world of dark bloody shapes. I think I was in the taverna last night with Gina and Nikki, but can't seem to remember exactly what happened.

I just went inside, but the only one around is this hag of a cleaning lady. I've gone upstairs looking for Gina, but she's not there. I've looked in every room and they're all empty. I'm trying to find out if the hag knows anything. I'm pointing upward, and as she looks back at me shaking her head from side to side I hear the mocking echo of my thoughts. I've got the hag by the shoulders. I'm looking right into her vacant black eyes, but I can hardly get the words out: " A girl . . . two men . . . a dancer."

Suddenly my mind is jolted with a wave of numbing memories and I'm reeling in nausea and disbelief. Just then, a wisp of a kid waving a mop pokes his head in from the back room and lets out an annoying whine. "You mean the American girl? The one they found upstairs all beat up and bleeding? They took her to the hospital."

I'm stunned, like I've been kicked in the head. I'm banging the kid up against the wall, screaming in his face, and through tears he tells me the hospital is a few blocks away, over on Apollonos, near Cathedral Square. The next thing I know, I'm running hard, dodging cars, knocking people over. By the time I reach the hospital my heart is jumping out of my chest. I'm gasping for air as I pound wildly on the wooden frame of the Emergency Room window, shouting like a maniac: "Gina Angelo. Gina Angelo. They brought her in last night. An American. The kid told me they brought her here!"

The impossible is happening. A tiny, gray-haired nurse has led me into a prayer chapel. There's a small wooden crucifix on the wall and a stained glass window of the Resurrection directly across from it. She sits down beside me on a long hard bench and, as two security guards watch my every move, she takes my hand and tells me that Gina is in serious condition. As the room starts spinning, I hear her voice trailing away as if she's speaking to me from the other side of the world. "Poor girl . . . she lost so much blood . . . she may even lose the baby."

I'm not quite sure what happened next, but I found myself banging my head against the wall and watching with a detached curiosity as blood began spurting over the nurse's white uniform. I heard my dwarf soul laughing at me as I lunged at the nurse. "Don't let them die. It was all my fault. I'm the one who should die." Then suddenly, one of the guards grabbed me from behind, and as we tumbled to the floor I felt a sharp crack at the base of my skull and began falling into a black hole of pain.

I don't know how long I've been unconscious. I feel as if I've been buried in a tomb of rock. I think I'm still inside the chapel, but it's dark, so dark I can't see my hands in front of my face. I can hear it raining outside, but it's raining so hard that it doesn't even sound like rain, it sounds like the growl of a great hungry beast. I am the hungry beast, and if it were possible I would rip out my guts and eat myself alive.

I've reached the very bottom of life where self-hatred has no limitations and the thought of death and emptiness fills you with a seductive sweetness. Finally, I see with total clarity what I had lost.

No, not lost, but thrown away out of vanity, and spite, and cruelty. For underneath all the aching loss and anguish was the specter of cruelty. I am the depraved monster who wanted to be free of Gina and the spark of life she carried. I had thrown love away, and now I wanted to destroy myself, and the cruel maddening memories which made my life an intolerable and unbearable burden. Yet even now, even in this desperate hour, I am certain that this blind stumbling in the darkness, this seeming betrayal of all that is good, must have happened for a reason. I believe this, even now, even when I have nothing left to believe in.

At that instant, I felt a wisp of wind touch my face like a gentle kiss, and once again I found myself caught up in the prayers of my youth. My soul was laid bare and I stood before my sins. I had been irresponsible, foolish, vain, and insensitive. I had been wrapped up in the Self, and through this act of Self-absorption had brought suffering and pain to those I loved. I had been given the gift of discernment and a call to a higher purpose, but the call had gone unanswered. Instead, I had succumbed to the pleasure of the senses and vanity of the intellect. Then, somehow, this all-consuming realization became an ecstatic moment of confession, and the surging distance between myself and God vanished.

I closed my eyes for what seemed to be a second, and when I reopened them, something so fantastic, so real, and yet so bizarre happened, that I could hardly believe what I was seeing. I don't even have the right words to explain it, but I must try.

The rain had stopped and light was coming in through the stained glass window of the chapel. But it wasn't daylight, it was something wholly different. Gradually, the walls, ceiling, and floor became enveloped by an effervescent, shimmering luminosity, until the entire chapel dissolved in translucent radiance. That's when I saw Gina as if she were right next to me. She was sitting up in a hospital bed, surrounded by an angelic aura that soon became so brilliant that it appeared as white fire. I could only gaze at it for an instant, but as Gina smiled serenely at me the brightness became a warm, healing wave of light, and in its engulfing radiance we became as one.

Suddenly, the air itself seemed alive with the most wondrous fragrance. It smelled like roses, but a thousand times sweeter, and then the atmosphere began to shimmer and vibrate. Just ahead, I could see a beautiful aura of luminous colors. The intensity of the light was dazzling, yet it did not hurt my eyes. Although I wanted to move into the translucent flow, I could not. Again, I gazed into the center of the penetrating aura and thought I saw someone gazing back at me.

Somehow, in a nonreflective flash, I understood that I was the source of the blissful light in which I bathed and the darkness in which I dwelt. But before I could embrace the deeper meaning of this vision, it was gone. Gradually, after what seemed to be a few minutes, I could see a tall figure enveloped in radiant white light whose face was as familiar as my own. This was the Glorious Presence I had seen in my dreams and visions since I had been a little boy. No words can describe the joy I felt at this moment of remembrance and awakening. As I looked into a pair of radiant eyes, an illuminating voice poured into my being:

> "Listen and remember all the Words flowing through your heart and mind. There is nothing new to accept or reject. There is only to discover that which has always been.

> "Walk through the world as One. Those whose inner fire burns to lead - let them guide the nations in peace. Those whose inner fire burns to heal - let them make well the sick. Let the poet sing, and the philosopher express the order of things. Let each find his special way, for each way leads to the Truth.

"What you believe to be different faiths are but moments of the same present instant and the same Word spanning the breadth of human history. Just as the moment of Creation is but one burst of Light, the Truth is unchanging and is the same through all the manifestations of human life.

"You who have yearned for Truth and Rebirth, listen to your Inner Voice - it is the eternal Spirit/ Heart. This alone is true: You are resurrected, each of you, in the continuation of each other. There is no death, only the bursting of Life in each present moment of the Universe. Look with new eyes at each other and the Cosmos of Light.

"In your Age, you will gather up the Holy Words of the Illuminated Ones and bind together that which you call disparate. In doing so you will know each other as One and the Same. Open your hearts to all the holy ways of life and you will come to believe in the simplicity of the first truth: I am God and You are Me.

"The Enlightened Teachers and all the Prophets - in times past, in the East and the West, in places known to the many and in those known only to the few, in those faiths that are practiced and in those forgotten - these Great Ones spoke to you at different times and different places with words suited to your understanding, but they all spoke the same Truth.

"This is the time for a Union of the Faiths. There is no Death, only the renewal of Life, and in all that exists there is that which is Love. Embrace

113

each other as yourself and, in doing so, you will
come to your New Beginning. Now awaken, fill
your Soul with the fire of Truth and become a
Being of Light."

Suddenly I was engulfed by an eruption of intertwining
realities. There was a rush of ecstasy and a bolt of truth piercing
my heart. Flashes of insights cloaked in words were burning away
the Darkness. An illumination poured into my mind that was more
powerful and compelling than I can ever hope to describe. I knew,
without conscious reflection, that the Glorious Being standing
before me had guided me through many journeys and many
lifetimes.

The Cosmic Presence stretched out his hands and from each
of his palms emanated a pure beam of light. I saw Gina once again
beside me, and as the diamond rays touched her forehead, golden
circles manifested directly above her. In their mirror-like radiance
Gina's past lives were revealed. Then, all at once, I found myself
engulfed by the emanating rays and saw before me reflected
images of my own conscious evolution.

Many embodiments appeared before us, both masculine and
feminine, and in each life we sought to reach unification with the
Godhead - the primal ground of Cosmic Being from which Love,
Wisdom, and Perfection flow into the material dimension. Far into
the past I saw my real Self, my spiritual Self, utilizing one body
after another, and through all these incarnations I found myself
connected to Gina.

It was then that we were blessed by manifestations of the In-
Dwelling Presence of God. We saw shimmering Beings of Light
flying through the heavens, each brighter than a thousand suns,
and each took on a thousand wondrous shapes and forms not seen
before. Yet in all their indescribable diversity these Beings of
Spirit-Light were as One.

Then, somehow, these unbounded and multiform Beings
miraculously transformed into the Enlightened Guardians and

Prophets of Humankind. We trembled in amazement and awe as we found ourselves in the midst of Illuminated Beings of every race, culture, and religion. Our ecstasy was immeasurable and beyond all words of human description.

I'm not certain how long we dwelt in this state of inexpressible joy, but eventually I became aware of a singularly glorious voice that filled every cell of my being with a sound more beautiful than any imaginable instrument:

> "You have seen in the reflected image of your Being the Awakened Self of your past lives. In all your Transformations you have been linked together. In life after life, even as you wandered in the Darkness, you have always sought the Higher Truth.

> "Even now, as you try to sustain this moment of awareness, know that there are many trials before you. Along the way, each of you will receive training and instruction, but know that the source of all is the In-Dwelling Presence you call God.

> "Stand unafraid in the source of this Knowledge, and from it you will draw all the Protection, Wisdom, and Courage you will need to endure and overcome the challenges and obstacles you will encounter on your Journey of Becoming.

> "In your present lives you have suffered much. But through hope, love, and forgiveness, you have taken another step toward the Spiritual Realm. The Love that binds you is that of the Perfected Spirit, and you will find that in your present lives your work in serving the Light will reach its highest unity and purpose.

"Now close your eyes and sleep. When we meet again you will know me as your Secret Self, for in your mind is a reflection of Cosmic Consciousness.

"Like your deepest insights and intuitions, these revelations cannot be expressed fully through language, but I will shape them in the thought-forms that you have grasped in your moment of radiant clarity.

"Seek to understanding their meaning, meditate upon the insight cloaked in the words, take them into the secret place of your heart, and like the purest flame they will burn away the Darkness."

Oh, Sound of Glory and Blissful Light. What was this wondrous music singing in my soul and reverberating in my mind? Insights cloaked in words burning away the Darkness. A rush of ecstasy and the flash of intertwining realities. A bolt of Truth piercing my heart. A wave of Joy resounding through the Universe.

Then I no longer heard the voice as a sound, but as a feeling that reverberated in my mind and through every cell of my Being. It was a feeling that I had never consciously experienced in this lifetime; yet I knew it had always been inside of me and inside everyone who had ever lived.

Then there was another jolting flash, and another, and another, and then it was over, and I knew with unshakable certainty that the energizing and compelling Presence was gone! The surge of power and the feeling of being a part of something inclusive and extraordinary were fading. My miraculous vision had disappeared and I found myself back in the hospital chapel slumped over a wooden bench. Yet, the memory of the transforming experience still raced through my mind. The lingering words and thoughts became an explosion of mind-energy. Somehow, I found my pen and journal and began writing down page after page of recollections with a ferocious intensity.

As the words flowed automatically through my fingers onto the paper, my mind became a spinning vortex of images and ideas that soared beyond anything that logic and reason could explain. Then, with a jarring unexpectedness, the words stopped flowing through my fingers. It was over. The writing had ended. Though drained to the point of exhaustion, I read and reread the words I had written, trying to understand their awe-inducing meaning.

As I closed the journal and held it to my heart, I was almost afraid to think, as if that very act of reflection might end the incandescent stream of thoughts which exhilarated me with their exquisite power.

Had these thoughts and words really been put into my mind by an Illuminated Being? Had I really experienced a momentary unification with the Cosmic Consciousness? Then, like a prayer in the secret part of my heart, I heard a voice, and it sounded strangely like my own:

> "Each Generation that comes into Being has the power to transform the world . . . . Those who are given the most must do the most . . . . In all that exists there is that which is Love . . . . Fill your Soul with the fire of Truth and become a Being of Light."

My heart was racing with an uncontrollable energy. Was all of this an ecstatic hallucination? Was I going insane? I felt as if I were emerging from a cocoon; experiencing a metamorphosis; transmuting into a new life form. Then, suddenly, I felt myself succumbing to an exhaustion of body and spirit as if I were returning to the Cosmic Womb from which I had come. The world began spinning out of control and out of focus. My expanding mind was shrinking and I found myself alone, unimaginably alone, with my small, limited understanding. Yet as I lay there at the edge of delirium, my soul was flooded with an uncommon serenity which washed away the madness and transformed the dark masque of my life into a dance of joy. All my demons had been silenced, the angels had been set free, and I surrendered completely to a dream of peace.

How long had I slept? Was it for a few minutes or an eternity? Now, inexplicably, I was awake! A jolt of bright light suddenly brought me back to reality, and I found myself watching the sunlight streaming through the stained glass window of the hospital chapel. Out of the corner of my eye I could see the tiny, gray-haired nurse bending over me. As she helped me up, she reached deep into her pocket and took out a carefully folded piece of blue paper. Then, as she placed it in my hand, she whispered: "Peace be with you my child. Gina gave me this last night and asked that it be given to you in the morning."

My fingers trembled as I unfolded the paper and began reading.

My Love,

> *In your heart you know I love you, but the temptations of this life were difficult to resist and I am as much at fault as you. Do not hate me or yourself for what has happened. I pray that God will watch over you and help you find a way to stop the burning torment that fills your soul. Remember me, and know you are forgiven.*

Gina

As the note slipped from my fingers I found myself racing from the chapel after the nurse. I caught sight of her just as she was about to get into a crowded elevator.

"Please," I begged, tugging at her arm, "tell me what room Gina's in. You don't understand. Something amazing . . . something miraculous has happened to me. Something so wonderful that everything has changed. Please, please help me, I've just got to find Gina." Then, just as I was about to describe my transforming vision, she touched me softly on the hand and said, "I'm so sorry . . . Gina's not here anymore . . . She's gone." The nurse still seemed to be speaking to me, but my mind was reeling. "Do you understand? When the doctors examined Gina this morning and saw her condition was stable, they signed her out. Gina's left the hospital; but she's going to be fine . . . and she's going to have a baby."

As the nurse turned and the elevator door closed behind her, I felt as if I had descended into a dense fog. I didn't even realize that two security guards were leading me out of the hospital until I found myself standing on the sidewalk in the rain. I felt as if I couldn't move, as if my legs had been planted in the ground; and I remained in that motionless daze for what seemed to be hours, replaying in my mind all that had happened in the past few days. I had committed horrid and detestable acts, and almost destroyed Gina. I had been beaten and almost driven mad, and yet, somehow, received a wondrous transforming vision that had given me a touch of illumination and understanding.

As I slowly began inching away from the hospital the sun broke through the clouds, and as I walked toward a dazzling rainbow I experienced a growing sense of renewal, as if I had been asleep and now had reawakened the memory of true intentions, sensing at the edge of understanding the essential reason for my existence. At that moment, my eyes filled with unexpected tears of joy, for I knew in my heart that Gina and I had been given the miraculous gift of life anew. Yes, we had suffered much and been scorched by the fires of madness and ecstasy, but through it all we had never given up on each other. We had survived, and now we were ready to withstand any challenges and obstacles we might encounter on our journey toward enlightenment. This time, I knew we would not make the same mistakes. This time, it would be different. Yet, I realized that even after all we had undergone and experienced, we were still at the very beginning of our journey. I knew without conscious reflection, in a way I could not fully comprehend, that Gina and I had always been linked together. Our souls were united like the twin arcs of the rainbow and we would always remain that way.

Something at the core of my being had changed, and now I could hear the music of truth in my heart and in my soul. I still had many unanswered questions, but I knew I had undergone a life-altering transformation that was leading me toward a higher plane of spiritual existence. I wasn't sure where I was supposed to go, or exactly what I was supposed to do, but with each tremulous step I became more aware of the profound beauty and sacredness of life, and the certainty that in each human soul is the power to heal and the wisdom to forgive.

I had been wandering aimlessly in the shadows, and my life had been a spiraling descent into disaster and disgrace. Now, I felt that my existence had been given a direction and a purpose, and I was possessed with the unshakable intuition that millions of other people around the world were experiencing a similar kind of spiritual awakening.

Suddenly, I heard a Glorious Voice singing in my soul, and saw a face smiling at me across infinity, a face that filled my soul with love. At that instant, I knew with unwavering faith that one day I would find Gina and our child. One day we would be together, and one day we would find our way back into the Light.

REPRISE

NOW

Many long years have passed since my spiritual awakening, and if I have told the tale well, it belongs to you. It has linked us together in an unbreakable bond and our lives have become one interconnected moment. Together we have lived through the terrors of the night. We have been scourged by the briars, barbs, and brambles of doubt, seen our fears fade, our hopes renewed, and given birth to a new consciousness. Have my words pierced your flesh and opened the wounds anew? Has your heart been filled with hope and your soul with an unquenchable thirst for truth? Do you believe that God is the breath, the heartbeat, and the spark of Self-Aware Mind that flows through Humankind?

At this very moment, I stand on a great cliff overlooking the Caribbean Sea in the ancient walled-city the Mayans called Tulum. Far below, two great rocks guard a small stretch of open sand; everywhere else the rock walls rise up creating an impassable fortress. There is a power here, an old and ancient power emanating from the rocks, the abandoned temples, the lush jungle . . . from even the tiniest pebbles, which heightens the senses. Something indefinable is at work here, something beyond ordinary awareness and understanding.

Night has fallen, and two stars shimmering like cat's eyes pierce through the blackness. The waves pound against the towering cliff and the wind whips the palms into a frenzy of celestial music. I can feel the subtle interconnectedness of things and the exhilarating sensation of life. In these living memories, I can see an almost unimaginable, interconnecting chain of wondrous events that brought me to Mexico, to the Yucatan Peninsula, where after years of tireless searching I finally found Gina and our miracle child. Together, as we stand before the all-encompassing waters I feel myself merging into the Cosmic Consciousness. My entire being is being transformed by love and truth, and a healing energy is flowing through my body replenishing me with an inexpressible and inexhaustible appreciation of life.

There is so much more I want to tell you. I want you to know of all the amazing adventures and struggles, of all the incredible events that eventually brought me to these sacred Mayan shores. But all of that must wait. My thoughts are turning into the poetry of dreams, and a Glorious Music in the center of my soul is filling my mind with thought-forms of radiant clarity. If you listen with an open heart, you too will hear and remember.

"Existence is One and Everything in it is Essential.

"The Human Mind transforms the Essential into the Rational and Irrational and gives order to the Manifestations through Thought-Forms.

"Matter in all its known and unknown forms, sentient and nonsentient, is Energy/Light. The Human Mind perceives matter as the Forms of Existence and gives Existence meaning through Pattern Recognition.

"God is the Ground of Disclosure. It is the name given by Humankind to the Totality of the Comprehensible and Incomprehensible Patterns of Existence. Humankind is an evolving, biological form of Living Matter with an evolving Discerning Consciousness (Spirit) that attributes purposefulness and intention to Itself, the Universe, and to God.

"Individual human life appears Finite and thus comprehends Matter in terms of a Cause and

Effect Nexus. Humankind cannot find the Cause and Effect of its Existence. Universal Anxiety results from Humankind's inability to find the Nexus of its Existence.

"The divergent Thought Systems of Religion assuage the Universal Anxiety of Humankind by initiating a set of moral, ethical, and social norms which derive their legitimization from the intuition of Oneness expressed in the lives of Illuminated Beings, which serve to raise the order of human relations to a level of Altruism that makes Civilization possible.

"The more successful a Civilization becomes in raising the order of human relations to increasing levels of Altruism and Harmony the more that Civilization intuits the Oneness of Existence and assuages Universal Anxiety.

"The Evolving Discerning Consciousness of Civilization rises to increasing levels of awareness as a Civilization becomes more successful in assuaging Universal Anxiety through Religious Thought Systems. As Discerning Consciousness evolves to higher states of awareness, Humankind has tacit knowledge of itself as an expression of the Oneness of Existence, and names this Love. Humankind exists as a biological form of Energy/Light/Matter and as an expression of Love, and its meaning and purpose is to bring Love into Self-Aware Consciousness.

"The realization of Love enables the Discerning Consciousness to evolve within the biological form and has been anticipated in History through the miraculous lives of Illuminated Guardians revealed as Prophets, Righteous Beings, and Teachers of the Holy.

"The realization of Love has been manifested in the Thought Systems of the Arts and Sciences as Genius and in the Thought Systems of Religion as Oneness with God.

"The differences in Religious Thought Systems exist because the intuition of the Oneness of Existence, expressed in the lives of the Enlightened Beings as the realization of Love, appears in diverse cultures at different historical moments.

"As each Culture, Language System, and historical moment is a unique manifestation, Religious Thought Systems differ in their Social, Philosophical, Ethical, and Ritual expressions. This differentiation over the course of the generations has divided Humankind, hindered the assuagement of Universal Anxiety, and diminished the awareness and capacity of the evolving Discerning Consciousness to realize Love and raise the order of human relations to ever-increasing levels of Altruism and Social Harmony.

"The recognition of these Thought-Forms by a critical number of Humankind will bring into History a Messenger who will divest the divergent Religious Thought Systems of their culturally bound differences, and bring into Self-Aware

Consciousness the essential recognition that Humankind is One People, that the expression of Oneness has a multiplicity of transformational forms embedded in the Planetary Genetic Pool, and that differences in Language and in the Thought Systems of the Arts and Sciences, Philosophy and Religion are expressions and manifestations of the Discerning Consciousness of an evolving biological form of Energy/Light/Matter as it brings the realization of Love to ever-widening circles of awareness in Humankind; and that the quest to give meaning to Existence is the reason for the Existence of Humankind."

ABOUT THE AUTHOR

Ivan Taub is an integral philosopher, playwright, and musician. Since 1997, he has been on the faculty of Temple University, where he teaches in the Intellectual Heritage Program. He holds a BA in religion, an MFA in theatre, and a Ph.D. in the humanities. He is currently working on Part Two of *The Messenger*, as well as a series of essays which explore the relationship between philosophy, science, and religion.

Printed in the United States
38069LVS00001B/136-168